Giraudoux

Three Faces of Destiny

ROBERT COHEN

Giraudoux

Three Faces of Destiny

THE UNIVERSITY OF CHICAGO PRESS

CHICAGO AND LONDON

Standard Book Number: 226-11248-9
Library of Congress Catalog Card Number: 68-29058

THE UNIVERSITY OF CHICAGO PRESS, CHICAGO 60637
The University of Chicago Press, Ltd., London

Printed in the United States of America

Aurélie: Il s'agit du monde.
Constance: De quel monde?

THE MADWOMAN OF CHAILLOT, ACT II.

Preface

This work is an attempt to analyze and evaluate the plays of Jean Giraudoux, whose popularity in this country has not yet been accompanied by an appropriate critical interest. While there is no attempt on my part to maintain that Giraudoux was a great original philosopher, I would like to show that his very stylized works are underlaid by an intellectual system at least as profound as those of dramatists more ostentatiously thoughtful, such as Sartre, Beckett, or Brecht. Thus I have organized the plays of Giraudoux according to the ideas which I find roughly central to them. The four sexual plays focus on domestic crises of a personal and sexual nature. They are, in my opinion, his weakest plays, and therefore the chapter that treats them may serve as an exposition for the rest of this study. The four metaphysical plays are fantasies that deal openly and directly with man's place in the universe. The four political plays demonstrate Giraudoux's concerns for society, and particularly French society and its future. These categories are not strict ones, for there are sexual, metaphysical, and political overtones in all of Giraudoux's work; however, I think it will prove both convenient and illuminating to see these particular plays side by side in this way. The four plays in each group are studied in the order in which they were written, and in each group a line of thought can be traced from play to play. The final chapter examines Giraudoux's style, particularly in relation to what he was trying to say and do with it.

I have kept this book entirely in English, or at least 99 per cent of it, even to the extent (which gave me a few shudders) of translating the titles of the plays, and anglicizing the names of many of the characters. Where I have had to use a French word or sentence, I have tried to make clear what it was all about. My reasons for this are or should be obvious—there are already a great number of good books about Giraudoux in French, and there is a scarcity of English studies. In addition, much of Giraudoux's work has not yet been made available in accurate English translations, and I have frequently contented myself with merely translating his own words in his defense, secure in the knowledge that this material has not heretofore appeared in our language, and has escaped the attention of a large number of people who would be interested in reading it. Naturally I have tried to translate as much of the feeling of the French into English as I was able, but above all I have tried to be accurate and impartial. One of the great hurts that has been sustained by Giraudoux's plays in America is a series of grossly altered "translations," which have been justified on the doubtful claim that this is necessary for "good theater." Having some experience in this field myself, I prefer Giraudoux's sense of theater to that of his adaptors, and I have tried to render it properly.

I have not discussed the adaptation *Tessa*, or the two films *La Duchesse de Langeais* and *Béthanie*, or the one-act *Supplément au voyage de Cook*, since they were neither germane to my central organization nor of sufficient independent merit to force a change in that organization. Available English translations or adaptations of Giraudoux's work will be found in the bibliography.

I wish to acknowledge my great indebtedness to the late John Gassner, who encouraged me to write this study, and to the University of California at Irvine, for providing the necessary assistance and stimulation. The chapter on "The Madwoman of Chaillot" was originally published in different form as "Some Political Implications of *The Madwoman of Chaillot*," in *Contemporary Literature*, Volume IX, Number 2 (© 1968 by the Regents of the University of Wisconsin).

Contents

Introduction

DESTINY AND HUMANITY

Jean Paul Sartre has said that Giraudoux writes in a code language. The comment was made in a rather unflattering article, which accused the then well established writer of "Aristotelianism," and said,

Up to now I have always tried to *translate* his works. That is to say, I have figured that M. Giraudoux had amassed a great many observations, and that he had drawn a wisdom from them, since he had, by his taste and preciosity, expressed the entire experience and wisdom in a code language. However, the attempts at decoding have never gained me very much: the profundity of M. Giraudoux is real, but it is valid for his world and not for ours.[1]

The simple factual observation of Sartre is correct; Giraudoux's plays are written in a code language and they admit a certain translation. When, for example, the Inspector in *Intermezzo* says, "Humanity . . . is superhuman!" a specific meaning of "humanity" is involved. When the words *destin* (destiny) *égoisme* and *fou* or *folle* (mad, madman, madwoman) appear, as they do over and over again, a specific language is involved. No study of the plays of Giraudoux can begin without some prior understanding of this language.

The key to deciphering the Giraudoux code is his own response to the rhetorical question, "What is tragedy?"

It is the affirmation of a horrible bond between humanity and a greater-than-human destiny; it is man yanked from his horizontal, four-footed posture and held erect by a leash; a leash whose tyranny is abundantly evident, but whose governing will is unknown.[2]

[1] Jean Paul Sartre, "M. Jean Giraudoux et la philosophie d'Aristote."
[2] "Bellac et la Tragédie," in Jean Giraudoux, *Littérature* (Paris: Grasset, 1941), p. 292.

This single sentence begins to express the underlying metaphysical structure of Giraudoux's entire dramatic work: a systematized division of the universe into two "worlds," and the tragic predicament of man "yanked" from one to the other. Man, at the outset, is born into a world of "destiny," a preconscious, prenatal state of tender sensations, animal instincts, and spiritual harmony. But he is soon "yanked" from this destiny, first by the doctor's forceps, then by society's strictures, into the cold, rational, mendacious world of "humanity," or human affairs. Literally, he is pulled upright to assume his role as a fully matured member of the world of humanity, and forced to forgo the more natural world of destiny below him. The tragedy in Giraudoux's scheme of things occurs when destiny tries to reclaim him.

To Giraudoux, man is an alloy composed of these two worlds, represented in him as his desire and his situation, the two joined inseparably by the heat of the conflict. Man's desire is to return to the world of destiny, the pure, unified, and comprehensible world where men marry the women they love, where girls enjoy spiritual communion with the dead, and where the eyes of a nation are limpid, honest, and beautiful. Man's situation, by contrast, is the world of humanity, which is crass, hypocritical, boring, and filled with ignoble compromises. Man finds himself pushed by his desires and pulled by his situation. In ordinary cases this simply makes him tired, uneasy, and frustrated. In the tragic state, it puts him at the breaking point, which Giraudoux frequently calls the point of *déchirement*, or tearing apart.

It should be emphasized that the creation of "worlds" was a literary, not a philosophic achievement. It allowed Giraudoux the creative options of theatrically creating the worlds, and indicating his tragic hero's plight between them. The code language is the verbal extension of the worlds. Two adjectives become part of the system: *égoisme*, which is the accusation destiny makes against humanity, and *fou* or *folle*, which is the accusation humanity makes against destiny. All of Giraudoux's great heroes are thus called mad, to wit: Ondine, Lucile, Judith, Isabelle, Electra, Hans, Apollo, and the best known of all, Mlle Aurélie, *la folle de Chaillot*. Their sublime madness is described in *Ondine*: "They have the reasoning of plants, of the waters, of God: they are mad" (III: 5). Egoism, by contrast, is the logic and practicality of human society. "Human knowledge . . . is at the most human religion, and it is merely a terrible egoism. Its dogma is to make impossible or sterile all ties with the non-human species" (*Intermezzo*, II: 3). "Destiny," "humanity," "egoism," and "mad" are all ideographs in the Giraudoux lexicon, outlining an intellectual and philosophical system which is the substructure of his dramaturgy. They never appear innocent of this larger context; they are always defining the tragic split between desire and situation. The details of these worlds will be elaborated in the discussion to follow.

Giraudoux did not, of course, write tragedies of an Aristotelian sort, and anyone familiar with his elegant style may well wonder at the aptness of his remarks on tragedy. There is a certain truth to Sartre's remark that his profundity "is valid for his world and not for ours." Yet Giraudoux's theater is more possible, in our times, than Aristotle's, and it has proved more viable than Sartre's. Giraudoux used his philosophical premises in an unconventional way. Rather than using theatricality as the vehicle to transmit a philosophy, he used philosophy to produce a theatricality. His theater has neither the classic catharsis nor the Sartrean message; what it communicates is the stylized form of theater itself. In this, Giraudoux's theater is the forerunner of theater of the absurd and the theater of cruelty. He did not write "tragedies," but he wrote plays *about* tragedy, and in doing so he created a glorious revival of the uses of the theatrical facility. It is important for us to see the intellectual integrity of this movement, since it is so deceptive that Giraudoux's plays have often been considered mere trifles. I appreciate the words of French film director Chris Marker in this respect:

Our accord with the entire works of Giraudoux, so full of playfulness, laughter, and glitter, is only made possible because of our complete confidence in the seriousness of his enterprise. But since his very gentility of spirit, which is levity with the gravest subjects, risks masking this seriousness from our view, it is we who must take the first steps.[3]

This study is an attempt to take those steps.

[3] Chris Marker, *Giraudoux par lui-même*, p. 13.

Judith—*1931*

Song of Songs—*1938*

Sodom and Gomorrah—*1943*

For Lucretia—*1944*
(*premiered 1953*)

One

THE SEXUAL PLAYS

To repeat: "Tragedy . . . is the affirmation of a horrible bond between humanity and . . . destiny; it is man yanked from his horizontal, four-footed posture and held erect by a leash."[1] This statement is Giraudoux's central one, and to it all his serious dramatic endeavours are related. None of his plays better illustrate his tragic disposition, however, than these four sexual plays, which directly trace man's "yank" from an idealistic world to the compromising world of humanity. The sexual plays deal directly with the relations of the sexes, and illustrate the antithesis between love (destiny) and marriage (humanity); also between libido (destiny) and necessity (humanity). Together they form a history of human disillusion and defeat.

The basic sexual dilemma that Giraudoux examines can be best seen in the Agatha subplot of *Electra*, "a little scandal inside the big one," where Agatha finds herself married to an aging and self-important diplomat called *le President*. As befitting a subplot, the lines are broadly and quickly drawn. Agatha realizes, like Ciprienne in Sardou's simple *Let's Get a Divorce*, that she's been had.

Agatha: I am pretty and he is ugly. I am young and he is old. I have spirit and he is an animal. I have a soul and he doesn't. And he is the one who has everything. In any case he has me. And I am the one who has nothing. In any case I have him. [*Electra*, II:6]

The story of Agatha runs parallel to the more vital story of Electra; the latter searches for social justice and the former for sexual excitement, and both courses lead to disaster. As a subplot, Agatha's story is hardly of more consequence than the traditional farce of Sardou, but as a theme for serious drama, particularly in *Judith*, *Song of Songs*, *Sodom and Gomorrah*, and *For Lucretia*, it has significance.

[1] See Introduction, n. 2.

These four sexual plays form a loosely connected tetralogy, which traces the story of one of Giraudoux's most famed archetypal characters, the young girl, or *jeune fille*. *Jeune fille* has a connotation of innocent wonder, beauty, and slightly old-fashioned exuberance, which totally escapes translation into English. *Judith* is the story of her broken virginity and loss of innocence, *Song of Songs* her transition into complacency and marriage, and her lament for a lost youth, *Sodom and Gomorrah* her disgust at marriage and earthly sex, and her flight into adultery, and *For Lucretia*, her ultimate repudiation of humanity by suicide. The tetralogy was written in this order, and has a planned continuity. These are Giraudoux's most pessimistic plays, almost devoid of the humor and theatrical gaiety which characterize his other works; philosophically they are naked structures. This seriousness has had two results: a relatively small popular appeal of the plays and a major critical interest in them. Though his prophecy is certainly erroneous, Georges May indicates the position of many critics when he suggests, "More than likely Giraudoux's future fame will thrive on *Judith* and *Sodome et Gomorrhe*, for they are the most unflinchingly devoid of concessions and compromises."[2] In fact, the sexual plays are simply less well realized theatrically than the fantasies, and while not more serious, have less in the way of diversions. In looking at the sexual plays, we are looking at Giraudoux's fundamental ideas in the raw.

Judith

Judith was first performed at the *Théâtre Pigalle* in 1931. It was Giraudoux's third play, following *Siegfried* and *Amphitryon 38*, and was his first to meet with less than tremendous success. Though not a commercial failure (it ran for forty-five performances, compared to 283 for *Siegfried* and 236 for *Amphitryon*), it drew a roasting from Parisian critics and, in turn, a rare reply from Giraudoux. The commotion was significant, for Giraudoux was making his first attempt at tragedy, and *Judith* is the only play he so designated on its title page. *Judith* was

[2] "Jean Giraudoux, Diplomacy and Dramaturgy," p. 94.

intended as an ideological tragedy. While Giraudoux's earlier plays had contained their fireworks in bloodless events and personalities, *Judith* combines precious disputations with a brutal, charnal tone; for example:

Prophet: Judith! Judith! Save us!
    (Jean throws him on the ground and kills him.)
Jean: There! You're saved! [I:9]

Judith must stand or fall as a tragedy.[3]

The story is one that was familiar to the author for a long time. In *Siegfried*, three years earlier, Giraudoux had his heroine compare herself to Judith, and ask for a confidante "as playwrights give to Judith or Charlotte Corday" (II:1). He possessed a list of nineteen earlier dramatizations of the biblical legend, including Hebbel's *Judith* and Lepetit's *Episodes de la Bible*.[4] How many of these he had read we can only surmise, but the story has features of obvious appeal to a dramatist interested in ideologies. It opposes religious and political antagonists within a florid historical framework, a combination which has been particularly enticing to modern dramatists.[5] And it has archetypal importance in human civilization. Giraudoux exploits the Judith legend with the abandon of a true theatricalist; his version of the story is no more consonant with its source than *The Trojan War Will Not Take Place* is with Homer.

The play is written in three rather uneven acts, and while the action occurs within a classically correct twenty-four hours, each act exists independently. Each describes a step down the path to adulthood for the *jeune fille*. Judith, of course, is the heroine and the symbol at the same time.

Egon: Speak, *jeune fille*. What is your title?
Judith: Just that.

She is an archetype and proud of it. The steps of her adventure with heroism, with sexual surrender, and with sainthood, are simple ones.

[3] The time may have come for *Judith*. The 1965 revival in New York by the Association of Producing Artists was both a critical and popular success. Rosemary Harris, as Judith, was able to add the sensuousness and vitality to the role which earlier actresses, apparently, had lacked.

[4] The complete list is in *Cahiers de la Compagnie Madeleine Renaud—Jean-Louis Barrault*, no. 36 (1961), pp. 105–8.

[5] Without any attempt at completeness, note Shaw's *Saint Joan*, Brecht's *Galileo*, Bolt's *A Man for all Seasons*, Anouilh's *Becket*, Eliot's *Murder in the Cathedral*, Osborne's *Luther*, Pirandello's *Henry IV*, Sartre's *The Devil and the Good Lord*, etc.

What Giraudoux does with them is to tear them into diverse and conflicting motivations and substeps, then put them back into the dramatic pattern. The result is a brilliant cacophony.

Judith's first step is her sacrifice. She has been chosen by the people in the streets to represent her race to Holofernes: to fulfill the prophecy, sleep with the assaulting general, and save her city from disaster. All that is demanded is her virginity. This is the *jeune fille's* prize; having it, even the Madwoman of Chaillot is at heart a *jeune fille*. Virginity is rarely a subject for serious dramatic concerns, but it is vital in the Giraudoux structure of life. The good whore, Suzanne, begs Judith not to make the sacrifice:

Suzanne: Oh Judith! In becoming a woman we don't simply change our state: we change our sex, our race. I want to preserve the miracle that is Judith—*jeune fille*.

Virginity is not physical but metaphysical; it is a link with an earlier race and the world of destiny. When it is lost, it can never be claimed again, and its loss signifies the demise of the *jeune fille*.

To Judith her virginity is "a promise locked in me like a child, the promise of the most beautiful defeat, the proudest shame" (I:8). It is a promise which must be given up, but cannot be given up lightly. She is disgusted by the hypocrisy of the Rabbis who force her to Holofernes' bed, and the stupidity of her fiancé, John, who refuses to support her. Virginity is too important to be sacrificed to the Jews; if it needs be sacrificed, she reasons, let it be for glory. "I am not the only *jeune fille* who has acted with her beauty and purity as if she was preserving them, not for a man, but for a great moment in the world," she says (I:5). Her decision to leave for Holofernes' tent—the subject of Act I—is based on pride, not selflessness. If she must sell out, she will at least name her price, and it is a high one.

Judith is carnally motivated. She is impetuous; moved more by adolescent fervors than the claims of rationality:

John: You are young, Judith!
Judith: What more will I know, being older? [I:5]

John tells her the lessons maturity brings. He describes the nature of existence in the world of humanity: "Everything pleasing to the soul soon passes in this base world, joy, friendship, victory; everything except defeat" (I:5). This is not a lesson that a pure-minded *jeune fille* can be expected to ingest without revulsion. Head high, she heads off to the unknown destiny which awaits her in Holofernes' tent.

Act I describes the motivational transition between *jeune fille* and *jeune femme*, and Act II leads up to the moment of physical, actual transition. In Act II the internal dialectic gives way to an external debate, with the chief figures being Holofernes and Judith. On entering his tent, Judith is humiliated by his guards and rescued by Holofernes. "Let's begin the comedy again, this time in truth," he says as he sends the others away (II:3).

Holofernes is not at all as the Jews had pictured him, he is "like only the king of kings can permit himself to be in this age of Gods: a man completely of this world, of *the* world" (II:4). He offers Judith, in place of a God who has deserted her, the joys of life, nature, and, above all, sexual pleasure. "You know perfectly well," he tells her, "that at certain times one can only regain a foothold in the supreme emptiness through pleasure. You are looking for it now" (II:4). Carefully he outlines the ethics of eudaemonism and atheism:

Holofernes: You have guessed it.
Judith: Guessed what?
Holofernes: That there is no God here.
Judith: Where's "here"?
Holofernes: In these thirty square feet around us. This is one of the rare places of truly free human beings. The gods infest our poor universe, Judith. From Greece to India, from North to South, there is no country where they don't pollute the air with their vices, their smells. The atmosphere, for those of us who enjoy breathing, is the barracks-room of the gods. But there are still some places where they are forbidden, and only I know where to find them. . . . I offer you for a night this villa on an airy, pure ocean. . . .

Holofernes' offer may not be the first that ever enticed a girl to part with her virginity, nor is it based on particularly novel grounds, but its expression is almost religious—what priests call unholy:

Holofernes: Think of breakfast in the morning served without a promise of hell, of tea in the afternoon without mortal sin, with a nice lemon and an innocent, scintillating pinch of sugar. Think of young men and young girls embracing in clean sheets and tossing the pillows at each other, . . . without angels or demons looking on! Think of man as innocent. . . . I offer you, for as long as you would like, simplicity and quiet. I offer you your vocabulary as a child, the words of cherries and raisins, in which you will never find God like a worm. I offer you the musicians you hear, who sing songs and not canticles. . . . I offer you pleasure, Judith. Before that tender word, you will see Jehovah disappear. . . . [II:4]

Holofernes' magic incantation works on Judith, and his magnificence, seen against the fitful torpidity of the Jews, excites her to sexual frenzy. It is a rare moment for the "precious" Giraudoux:

Holofernes: Your body tells me . . . that it wants to be caressed, to be adored, to be touched by my lips, by the palm of my hand, my forehead, the forehead of a king. It protests. It wants to be God. You, what do you want?
Judith: To be insulted, to be plundered. [II: 5]

Judith goes to the fated bed of Holofernes with both passion and misgiving. She is still, in the second act, all potential. Holofernes tells her, "Only tomorrow will you know if you are miserly or lavish, if you are angelic or shrewish. You do not know today. From my bed you will arise pregnant with your first child: yourself" (II: 7). Judith the virgin has still to make her transition. She goes to Holofernes amidst confusion, expecting "something between crucifixion and mad laughter, between a nettle sting and death" (II: 8). There is one thing she knows, however: that Holofernes is "the first man who has ever moved her heart" (II: 6). Thus her initiation into womanhood, despite the biblical and political trappings, is nothing more than that of any young girl's first sexual experience. The tragedy is about to begin.

The final act is the attempt to define the action that has taken place. Judith returns from Holofernes' tent at dawn, leaving the king murdered in his bed. The troops of Holofernes are dispersed when shown the dead king's head, and the Jews rejoice and begin to sanctify "Saint Judith." But there are two conflicting explanations of Judith's behavior. Joachim, chief rabbi of the Jews, stands behind "God's truth," which is that Judith acted from hate, slaying her country's enemy in a selflessly heroic act to save the nation. But Judith refuses to be swept along with "God's truth," and gives her own version. According to Judith, she killed for love. Her thought had been to kill herself as well, but she could not withdraw the dagger from Holofernes' corpse. More importantly, she loved Holofernes, and she loved her night with him. When Joachim's singers start to chant Judith's praises, and suggest that Holofernes never "took" her, she interrupts them brusquely:

Judith: He did take her. And he had never been so strong, and she was so filled by him that there was no room left in her anywhere, not even for God. [III: 5]

The Jews are scandalized. The "heroinely" deed was not, apparently, performed in a "heroinely way," and it would be unthinkable for them to have to base their salvation on an act of wantonness. Yet Judith insists on giving her own version of what had happened the night before:

Judith: Stop your Jewish behavior of embalming lies in canticles. Listen to the truth, and its simple words. Yes, a Jewess lay down with Holofernes that night—in joy. . . .

As for the joys of the bed—she exhausted them, and asked for them, right up to the end. And at the first chill of dawn she piously drew the sheet over Holofernes as she would for her husband . . .

And between her people and Holofernes she chose love, that is to say, Holofernes, and ever since, one sole idea has appealed to her: to rejoin him in death. [III: 5]

This is "Judith's truth." To protect it, she has buried it in a drunken sleeping guard, whispering it in his ear so he will repeat it when he awakens. The Jews are outraged, and Judith is besieged by the rabbis to change her story.

Which is she, heroine or whore? And which "truth" is to be believed, God's or Judith's? Giraudoux adds two twists to the tale. First, God's messenger appears. He is in the person of the same sleeping guard to whom Judith whispered her secret. Now, as he rises, the Rabbis suddenly are frozen in midgesture, and he speaks directly to Judith, and only to her. He tells her that God has been with her all night, guiding her way, inspiring her with hatred, weighing down upon her dagger. He claims that he and the other angels acted as a hermetic sheet between Holofernes and her through the night, a mammoth prophylactic which kept her virginity technically intact. He claims that God acted through her subconscious, and through her passions— by his presence rather than his stated command. And he orders Judith back to her people to assume the burdens of sainthood. He threatens her, throwing her to the ground in a single gesture. Judith is forced to accept the order of God. "Be satisfied, I will follow you," she tells the Rabbis, who are suddenly revived (III: 8).

In the final moments of the tragedy, Judith relinquishes her friends and family, all hopes of love and happiness. "My mouth is dry . . . my body is dry," she tells the rabbis (III: 8). She will henceforth live in the synagogue and be the high judge of the Jews. But the sleeping guard adds a final turn to the plot. As Judith prepares to leave with the rabbis, one puts a black cloak on her:

Paul: It goes well on the wife of God.
Guard: (dead drunk) And on the widow of Holofernes. [III:8]

Insistently, the guard drunkenly exclaims what Judith had told him before, "She killed for love." Judith orders his tongue to be cut out, but the guard becomes a mimic:

Judith: What madness is this?
Paul: I don't understand what he's miming with that kiss!
Guard: What I'm miming? I'm miming Judith the whore. [III:8]

Judith orders him killed. Now she turns to her cortege. "Judith the saint is ready," she says as the curtain falls.

Again, is she Judith the whore or Judith the saint? This is the fundamental question of the play. Which is the "real" Judith? A dialectic, the fundamental weapon of Giraudoux's dramaturgy, is set up. By dialectic it is simply meant that two opposing and irreconcilable forces, destiny and humanity, are set at each other's throats without resolution. The dialectic itself defines the character: Judith is neither whore nor saint, nor middling creature between them; she is the product of both of them, she is defined by the dialectic of her personality. So, for that matter, is Holofernes, the rational sensualist. "Two Holofernes! Two Judiths!" he cries (II:5). The outside world can pin on Judith whatever label they wish, whichever "truth" appeals to them. But motivations, in Giraudoux's dialectical universe, are never single; they are dual. Judith, driven by destiny, kills Holofernes for God and for justice; yet, also driven by humanity, she loves the sexual adventure which precedes the killing.

"The crowd knows God's truth. Judith's truth is of little importance to them. In a few minutes, the two will be confused," says Joachim (III:5). Neither Judith nor Joachim know "why" she did what she did; the only certainty is the event itself. The "real" truth is in the action, and its motivation will always be multiple and therefore ambiguous. Giraudoux demonstrates that the doer of an act (Judith) is no more able to define it than the observer (Joachim), and that the motivation for any human act is embedded in the subconscious and the obscure. Human action is the result of urgings and restraints of which we are only dimly aware, even when they affect ourselves, and Giraudoux's natural response is an existential one: that the motivation and the action are identical; and that an act, being tangible, cannot be precisely defined by words, which are abstract. "Motivations," after all, are merely words, and words are useless instruments of moral evaluation in a world where the rabbi's "God, from a thousand years away, projects saintliness onto sacrilege and purity on lust" (I:7). *Judith* does not take us back to the fairy-tale land of Bible stories, it catapults us into the pagan void of *Job*.

It is an odd but pertinent paradox that, in *Judith*, the forces of the worldly are the most spiritual, and the forces of religion the most mundane and hypocritical. Holofernes, the barbarian, is the representative of all that is childlike, sensual, tactile, and honest (destiny); Joachim, the Rabbi, is the embodiment of compromise and hypocrisy (humanity). The God of *Judith* is a rapacious Old Testament patriarch, who yanks the leash of observance around the necks of his chosen people, and does not disdain to administer the lash when necessary—as demonstrated when the Guard throws Judith to the ground to emphasize God's will (III:7). The God of *Judith* is not, however, metaphysical. He represents himself only through a bureaucracy of rabbis, messengers, and prophets. His intrusion into man's affairs is the intrusion of humanity rather than destiny, the intrusion of practical politics. God, in this existential world, is merely the weapon of the rabbis. *Judith* is a play which admits of God's existence, but not his intellectual or ethical superiority. It leaves for man's secular consideration the determination of ethics and the nature of human existence.

Giraudoux is concerned, in *Judith*, with the ethical considerations of motivation. Is Judith less a heroine insofar as she is also a whore? Implicit in the Judith legend is that the sexual surrender was merely a distasteful means to an end; in reversing this, Giraudoux throws the entire moral lesson of the original into doubt. Motivation is not merely a matter of arbitrary definition in social life. Law distinguishes premeditated murder from the unpremeditated as a very different crime; so does history. This means that, in order to determine what someone has done, it is necessary to determine what he thought he had done. In a purely existential world such abstract investigations could be dispensed with, but neither our world nor Judith's behaves in that way. *Judith* poses an ethical dilemma based on one or another version of an observable deed, and the conflict between the versions is permanent. *Judith* explores this dichotomy between outward and inward motivations, and bears down on the impossibility of resolving them.

More broadly, the play describes the first transition in adult life: the voyage from destiny to humanity as the *jeune fille* passes into womanhood. As Judith is followed down the woody path to Holofernes' tent, so is she followed on the eternal path from *jeune fille* to *jeune femme*; that is, from an essential and defined world, past an exquisite moment of stillness and calm, then on to a new world which is chaotic and existential. Words and definitions now mean nothing, and systematized values are debased. This is the "tragedy" of Judith, which only on its surface has a happy ending. "Young girls are made for monsters, beautiful and hideous, but they are given to men. From then on their lives are wrecked" (II:7), says Holofernes, pointing to the true subject of the play, the innocent youth inexorably yanked by the world of humanity and its components: old age, ugliness, mediocrity, and hypocrisy; and the foretold failure of human life to achieve its desired destiny. The *jeune fille* is, unfortunately, defined not only by her present but by an inevitable future:

Judith: You know what *jeune fille* is?
Egon: It's what Sarah [a procuress] used to be. It's what all whores and
madams used to be. . . . It's a future *femme*, [i.e., wife/woman] ready
for the grotesque shames which will make her a *femme*. [II:2]

Judith is the tragedy of man's fall from innocence and his acceptance of defeat; it is an autobiographical, human tragedy and not merely concerned with the fate of young girls. The girl is merely a symbol. "Such is Judith, first in her class, chosen of God," says the Guard (III:7). As a young man Giraudoux was always the first in his class, and he was perpetually the one young man "chosen" for scholarships in the capital, at the École Normale Supérieure, and at the Sorbonne. *Judith* traces his, and every man's, forced removal from that ego-centered, promise-filled destiny of youth, and knocks us, along with his Judith, off our pedestals of purity, innocence and potentiality.[6]

The crystalline moments of youth are those which become most inaccessible after man's acceptance of adult civilization, and Giraudoux's

---

[6] There is a very interesting, comparable action in T. S. Eliot's *Murder in the Cathedral*, a nostalgic glimpse of a childhood victory repudiated by mature realization: "The prizes given at the children's party, the prize awarded for the English Essay, . . . all things become less real." We can see the fourteen-year-old T. S. Eliot accepting his prize for the English essay, and a twelve-year-old Giraudoux placing first in his class at the 100 meter dash (and we must recollect something like that in ourselves) and we feel the futility of adult life, which fails to give such meaning to its victories.

efforts were directed at recapturing them, if only for a fleeting second. It was an effort of his life as well as his literature. A friend records this conversation, and comments upon it:

> [*Giraudoux*]—How old are you?
> [*Beucler*]—Twenty-six.
> [*Giraudoux*]—Twenty-six years already! Hold on to them. Is there very much youth left in them?

> He was the only man who could let himself talk like that—with a light tone—of life, which passed all too quickly from its first day. And I could see with a certain terror the importance he attached to fresh impressions, to the naïve years, when everything was engraved with profundity, to the first moments of existence, where all was full of mystery and the promise of mystery.[7]

Harold Clurman passes on a suggestion that *Judith* is a parable of Giraudoux's own life, divided between duty to the state and his desires to be a poet.[8] But *Judith* is more fundamentally autobiographical than that. It is a description, in ways a grimly tragic celebration, of the defeated promises of youth, the passing of a childish delight in innocent and irrational pleasures (Holofernes' "child's vocabulary, a language of cherries and raisins,") and the ossification of the body and spirit in a dry civil world. "My body is dry," is Judith's final capitulation into womanhood, and representative of man's acclimatization to the world about him.

The relative failure of *Judith* in its original presentation was easy to predict, and the play has enormous difficulties which must be overcome in production. It is primarily a drama of classification; that is, the audience is asked to do nothing but choose the proper adjective with which to describe the heroine, a problem that is wholly semantic. Further, the problem is left unresolved. *Judith* is brilliantly ironic but rather poorly realized theatrically, particularly in view of Giraudoux's previous successes on this score. It was his first attempt to write a naked, personal tragedy, a genre that had then been relegated to the naturalists, and it was not a success. Yet its worth, like the other three sexual plays that were to follow, exceeds its dramatic limitations. It is a luminous window into Giraudoux's thought.

---

[7] André Beucler, "Vie et mort de Giraudoux," p. 109.

[8] Introduction to *Jean Giraudoux, Plays* (London and New York: Oxford University Press, 1963), vol I, p. xii.

Song of Songs

Song of Songs[9] is an urbane lament for that adjustment to the civilized world, specifically the adjustment to marriage. The comedy was Giraudoux's sole contribution to the repertoire of the *Comédie Française* (1938), Jouvet then being a director at the famed theater, and its brilliant brittle irony was perfectly suited to the polished comedians of the "House of Molière." It is a wiser and more compassionate play than *Judith*, being at once less passionate and more subtly alive.

The story is a modern one, though the inspiration is biblical. "For it came to pass when Solomon was old that his wives turned away his heart," says the Old Testament (1 Kings 11:4), and this is Giraudoux's theme, reconstituted in a Parisian cafe sometime following the Stresa Conference of 1935 (which is mentioned in the text). Giraudoux's "Solomon" is a character who appears in *Electra, Madwoman of Chaillot* and *The Apollo of Bellac*; he is "the president," a worldly-wise diplomat who in this play somewhat resembles Giraudoux himself.

He is "the most stubborn orator in Europe" (Scene 1), the man who, like Giraudoux, had helped negotiate the German peace after World War I, and the ill-fated French-British-Italian Alliance at Stresa. He is more than a man, he is part of a "race" of presidents:

President: Who are you looking for?
Chauffeur: You, Monsieur le Président. Monsieur le Président has sent me for you. [Scene 8]

The president waits at his table for his beautiful mistress, Florence, but their rendezvous turns out to be their adieu. Florence comes with her new lover, a simple, good-looking young man named Jerome, who proudly announces that he and Florence are engaged to be married. It is a story older than Solomon, no doubt, but one in which Giraudoux has injected novelty, wit, and verbal brilliance. Giraudoux interprets the biblical statement, and finds it is not merely a question of their age which sends young girls flying into the arms of young men, it is a matter of destiny. In the earlier play, Judith had told the singers to "stop . . . embalming lies in canticles" (III:5), and this *Cantique*

---

[9] *Cantique des Cantiques.*

des Cantiques is an attempt to uncover one more misunderstanding codified in biblical myth.

The protagonist of the play is Florence, not the president. She is the character in transition, the one whose decisions become the pivotal moments of the play. Florence is one step beyond Judith: no longer a virgin but not yet a wife, she is called a *jeune femme*; in fact, "the most charming of *jeunes femmes*" (Scene 1). Her transition from *jeune fille* to *jeune femme* was years past, when the president had given her a pearl at the dinner table at a resort hotel in Aix, where they were sojourning. "The maître d'hôtel was furious. . . . He had been looking after me. . . . Suddenly he noticed that pearl on my left hand. He was sure it hadn't been there five minutes before. He had called me *mademoiselle* when he brought the wine. He called me *madame* when he served it" (Scene 6).

Now it is time for Florence to make the subsequent transition: from mistress to wife, that is, from *jeune femme* to *femme*. The play becomes her lament for the loss of her youth and freedom; her leave-taking of the sensual pleasures of a happy and uncomplicated affair, and her acceptance of mundane ordinariness in marriage. "He [Jerome] touches me and everything in me becomes dry," wails Florence (Scene 6), using the same metaphor for marriage as Judith had for sainthood; both being reconciliations to the adult, societal world. The transition is not an easy one to make, and Florence's body rebels from it. She begs the president to take her away, but he, sensing destiny at work, refuses:

The President: No. I can't. I am the only man in Europe who knows when he's beaten.

Florence: He is probably beautiful, but I can't see him. He is probably good, but his goodness escapes me. He is probably generous, but I never get anything from him. Take me away, Claude!

The President: It's not you talking. It's the lamentation beginning again.

Florence: You mean my *lamento*?

The President: Yes. Your song. I am listening to it. It is beautiful. It is reason itself. You would be crazy to think that you came here today for anything else but to sing it. . . . But how can I tell at this moment whether you are crying in grief or ecstasy? [Scene 6]

The *lamento* is Florence's "Song of Songs," of course—neither grief nor ecstasy, but both combined in a grim celebration of fate, a tragic ode to the inevitable course of birth, copulation (marriage), and death.

Florence has no actual choice between Jerome and the president.

Hers is the story of the "yank" whose force we feel and whose authorship we know not; marriage is simply a part of the inexorable process. Jerome is the instrument of a young girl's fate, and her marriage to him was destined from afar. "He came from a long way away. He was sent off twenty years ago" (Scene 4). He has the attractiveness of a creature of destiny: purity, honesty, and a youthful beauty. He is an "*être pur*" (Scene 5), a "kind of archangel." Florence speaks of his blank innocence: "He has the candor of monsters. He is without suspicion. He is ignorant of good, of bad, ... of conquest, of defeat. He is ignorant of everything" (Scene 4). But Jerome's innocence is malignant in a civilization which is not as pure as he is. His silence is like that of a cellmate that jailors put in the cell of a prisoner from whom they wish to extract a confession:

Florence: He is there, like them, indifferent, friendly. He eats my food. He washes with my water. He sleeps in my bed. He hardly bothers to talk. He is waiting for me to confess.
The President: Confess what?
Florence: My happiness before knowing him. My complicity with so many beautiful things, so many wonderful people whom I esteemed, whom I caressed. [Scene 4]

However, Jerome is not a creature of destiny. He is terribly ordinary, a silly child who has learned electrical repairing and soldering and will earn his living fixing watch chains and short circuits. Florence calls him the "god of little metals" (Scene 4) as opposed to the more substantial president. "With you it is oil, gold, and iron," she tells the president, "with him it is celluloid, chrome, glass, lacquer, and aluminum" (Scene 4). There is nothing divine about Jerome, nothing of destiny. The impulse to marriage, Giraudoux indicates, transforms its protagonists into superhuman mirages. Jerome, the watch-chain repairman, becomes Tristan in the eyes of Florence's Yseult. "I don't love him," she acknowledges, "that's evident. But I do *love*, don't I?" (Scene 4). Blind love is the demigod from destiny, which relentlessly impels man, blighting his rational values.

From the realistic point of view, the president is a far better match for this *jeune femme*. He is kind, wise, gentle, and handsome. He is exceedingly generous. And he loves her as well—more than Jerome ever will. The waiter, the cashier, and even the manager of the café (all of whom overhear the proceedings) totally favor him over his younger rival. Giraudoux favors him, giving him the same heroic attributes—

pitilessness and tenderness—that he gives to Hector in *The Trojan War*, and that he had given to himself.[10] Even Florence favors him. But she can do nothing about it, nor can anyone else. She falls back on reciting her Song of Songs:

Florence: You know women. I was suddenly taken with the desire to lament, to lament from my depths, from my entrails. Like a need to stretch myself, to cry, to sing. That's it, to sing. I had a melody in my head, a pathetic melody.... The gayest woman one day will cry out in her despair, the happiest woman her distress. It is a function of the body, not of the soul. I have absolutely nothing to do with it. [Scene 6]

Florence, her *lamento* ended, goes off to marry Jerome. She returns to the president the jewels he had given her, "our armor," as she refers to them (Scene 6). But she cannot give back what she truly must. The president tries to persuade her to keep the jewels but give up that one thing:

The President: To stay opposite Jerome you will need a core: a secret, a treasure.
Florence: I have one, I love you.
The President: You can see where that will lead! That's exactly what you must get rid of. [Scene 6]

But she does not. Love, once truly given, will never completely disappear, and innocence, once abandoned, will never be totally reclaimed. The memories of past freedoms and happiness will haunt this marriage to its end. "I will always carry it in my thoughts," says Florence of the pearl the president had given her at Aix (Scene 6). The future of her marriage to Jerome cannot be a happy one:

Florence: You see what I'm suffering, what I have suffered....
The President: And what you are going to suffer. [Scene 6]

Like all of this series, *Song of Songs* describes a tragedy of life. It is a religious celebration. The French title, *Cantique des Cantiques*, implies the ritualistic, hymnlike quality of the celebration more than the English title, *Song of Songs*, making the distinction between song (chant) and hymn (cantique) that Giraudoux implied was an important one.

---

[10] "You have a forehead, pitiless but tender," Florence tells him (Scene 4). "You are tender because you are pitiless," Hector says about himself in battle (*Trojan War*, I:3). "Already I was pitiless and tender," said Giraudoux about himself in *Adieu à la Guerre* (Paris: Grasset, 1919), p. 12.

Thus Holofernes had offered Judith, in the earlier play, "musicians who sing songs and not canticles" (III:4). In offering us this time a canticle, Giraudoux is offering a rigid form, a structure. "I will only remember the melody," says the president (Scene 6). He need not recall the words, since, in this play, it is the structure that is of first importance. This takes the story into the realms of the eternal far more than does its biblical title or historical setting.

Like all of Giraudoux's work, perhaps more obviously than most, *Song of Songs* is a metaphor, standing for that brief moment of transition between one state of being and another: Giraudoux speaks of it in a theatrical sense as an entr'acte between epochs, periods of time. The president tells the waiter at the beginning of the play, "I have come here because today I need an hour away from the world, over-looking it from a balcony of serenity" (Scene 1). And this is what the play gives him: a moment of removal, of objectivity, from which he can examine the pathetically whimsical human comedy. Soon he must plunge back into the human condition, but for a few moments, at his café, he can sit back and observe; it is "A moment of happiness, of peace, of intermission between the duties of the career, the family, and the nation" (Scene 1). This objectivity lends the work its unquestioned coolness, its metaphorical rather than subjective or realistic truth. But as the cashier in the play says, "the metaphor . . . is truth itself" (Scene 1).

The position of Giraudoux in *Song of Songs* is similar to that of his president's: objective, detached, and compassionate. Both are resigned to the inexorable course of a man's life and powerless to counteract the "yank." The resulting comment is a bemused and ironic one, with nothing to be done but step aside. "It's amusing to live—you'll see,"[11] Giraudoux once remarked to a younger acquaintance, and one senses that bittersweet feeling throughout this play. Defeat is inevitable, and the destiny of a woman's changing heart is foretold and foreordained. The philosophical structure is eternal; and Giraudoux's biblical references give *Song of Songs* an archetypal quality. Jerome, like the doe-breasted girl in the Bible, has "lips like a thread of scarlet," and one senses that the path of the *jeune femme* is a well-worn one.

Song of Songs lacks the bitterness of *Judith*, and it eliminates the dark tone that infused the earlier play. It scarcely uses the theatrical medium, and is in some respects Giraudoux's most conventional play. Much of

---

[11] André Beucler, "Vie et mort de Giraudoux."

this can be attributed to the fact that it was written to be performed at the *Comédie Française*, which was not then known for its hospitality to innovative works. But more probably Giraudoux simply had different things on his mind than the sexual dilemma. The time was 1938, and political activity was frantic. Hitler was in the Rhineland, in Austria, and battering on the doors of France. Giraudoux had just written *Electra* and was working on his political opus, *Pleins Pouvoirs*. The future of the French republic, to which Giraudoux had devoted a great share of his adult life, was in the balance. At the conclusion of *Song of Songs*, the president is called for by the president of the council. The president of the council had said, "while laughing, that it was a matter of saving the Republic" (Scene 8). In light of his other works, *Song of Songs* seems today an academic exercise. The sexual plays in general did not provide Giraudoux with his best material, and *Song of Songs* is probably the thinnest of all of them. But it forms an important link in the sexual tetralogy, treating the inevitable course toward marriage and aging womanhood with urbanity, compassion, and a genial wit. It is a comedy of profound sadness.

Sodom and Gomorrah

Judith describes the path of the *jeune fille* between virgin and mistress; *Song of Songs* takes her from mistress and makes her a wife. Both plays forecast the suffering and misery of marriage; both stop short of portraying it. *Sodom and Gomorrah* is the result of the predictions of the previous plays; it is a bleak depiction of loneliness, deception, and bitter hatred in marriage. It was written five years after *Song of Songs*, and shows the deterioration of a five-year-old marriage. It is without question Giraudoux's least popular play. Although the gloom of Occupation can in part be blamed for the awesome tone of the drama, which was first performed in Paris in 1943, there is nothing in the play that is in the slightest way inconsistent with Giraudoux's developing ideology of love, sex, marriage, and death. The play is the third in this tetralogy, and its subject is the disharmony between marriage, an institution of humanity, and love, an ideal in human destiny.

God rained brimstone and fire upon Sodom, according to the Old Testament, because he could not find ten righteous men in the city. Further, the behavior of the Sodomites in respect to the two male angels visiting Lot was nothing short of scandalous; certainly it was worthy of divine retribution in those darkest of days. In Giraudoux's clarified and modernized version, God seeks not ten men or even one; he will save the city for the sake of just one couple. And the crime of Giraudoux's Sodomites is not the ancient one of buggery, but the failure of heterosexual love. Marriage, as a human institution, is on the point of collapse. The "couple" has divided; the men are in the north, the women in the south.

> The entire dowry of the couple, its faults and virtues, has been eagerly divided between the men and the women as jewels and furniture on the eve of their divorce. . . . They no longer have pleasures in common, memories in common, flowers in common . . . each sex secretes its own light, and what is worse, each secretes its own truth. [Prologue]

God makes it clear that there is only one couple left that can save Sodom: Jean and Lia. It is the familiar dramaturgic device of *Electra* and *Judith*: the city will be destroyed, "*unless* . . ." In this case the "unless" is: unless Jean and Lia can truly be found to be satisfied in marriage. As in *Judith*, the affair is personal rather than political. "The question God is posing is not of Sodom and Gomorrah, but of Jean and Lia" (II:5), says Lia, and the affairs of the city are merely the theatrical dressing of a personal, sexual tragedy:

Lia: The end of the world is only a stage setting, isn't it?
Jean: A detail of the setting for the end of the couple. [II:6]

Thus, *Sodom and Gomorrah* is a cosmic reaction to the housewifely question, "Can this marriage be saved?" Giraudoux's wry rephrasing is: "Can *marriage* be saved?" Marriage, like a many-faceted diamond, is slowly rotated in the Giraudoux luminescence—we can see it sparkle from all angles, but it cannot be penetrated.

The first aspect of marriage is its disillusion. Lia's five-year-old marriage, like her friend Ruth's, has already failed in its promise:

Lia: This is the lesson of marriage. All sorts of charms are posed on the one you marry. He is an elm abounding with finches which you gather in. Then, week by week, each finch flies off to another man, and at the end of the year your true husband is disseminated onto every other male in sight. [I:1]

Similarly, with Ruth and her marriage to Jacques:

Ruth: That man, pure as the day, the color of daylight, he was going to be
my joy, my constant adventure. With him, by him, I was going to
taste the delicacies and ecstasies of life which I would never have
enjoyed by myself. I was holding in my arms the one who was going
to love me, suffer for me. I was going to see on my body and my soul
all the bites and caresses of life. What a performance! What a future!
Lia: The performance never took place?
Ruth: You said it! [I:1]

For Lia, her husband has changed; he has lost all of his glory and individuality. For Ruth, her husband has remained exactly the same.
Actually the difference is negligible. In each case the women have
found themselves attached to boring, ordinary men, whom they would
rather find dead than alive. A frightful silence descends over marriage:

They touch each other with distaste. They look at each other with
mistrust. Their very shadows mingle in hatred. Perhaps a fight would
enlighten them. But it's time for lunch. [I:2]

The picture Giraudoux has drawn of marriage is a grim one, beginning in disillusion and ending in despair and death. Disillusion is first.
The *jeune fille* is led to marriage with bright hopes of glorious days and
marvelous nights, an unending communion of human souls. Lia is a
jeune fille past repair, uncompromised with reality, and in fiery rebellion against the leash. She is a true madwoman:

Jean: Pardon her, angel. She is mad.
Angel: No, she is right. [I:2]

Her madness is an unconverted purity. Like Judith, she is the definition
of herself: her name is her title. "My name is woman. My name is
love," she declares (I:4). And she is a woman from all centuries, an
escapee of Eden, purer than Eve:

Lia: Across the ages, across death, across the broad spectrum of madness and
wisdom, across the changing faces of the earth; my hands, my hips,
my eyes have told you of the devotion and the hope before the Fall.
All that you know of what were once true rivers, true trees, true life—
it has been by me that you have known them. [I:2]

Like true creatures of destiny, Lia is supported by her sister *jeunes
filles*, namely Judith, Salome, and Athalie. Judith, who speaks for the
others, tells Lia, "We are three or four who don't mind the heat"
(II:3). Creatures of destiny never do. Lia's drive is for a love so total

and overwhelming that it will destroy her in fulfilling her. Her demands of love are cataclysmic. Like Judith, who wants to be "plundered" by Holofernes, Lia demands of love the total commingling of body and soul. "Love is noble not when it exalts two beings as a model couple, but when it crumbles them together until they are dust," she tells her abashed husband (I:3).

But no human being is capable of such intercellular communication; the human organism is, in even the most intimate circumstances, self-centered. The very intimacy of marriage, with the physical and social intercourse of bodies, breakfasts, and memories, makes this failure of communication particularly noticeable and especially tragic. The illusions shatter. Lia's search is aborted. Reality descends:

> Lia: Inhabitants of earth are separated by a terrible window. Don't you
> realize that I would have been satisfied with just a man? Let me reach
> him, let me touch him, that's all I asked, and God knows I rubbed at
> Jean's window, I hit at it, I scraped it. It remained intact. [I:4]

It is not merely a matter of Jean and Lia. Lia admits that the same impenetrable window encases Jacques, and that adultery with every man in town ("Jean" and "Jacques," in French have the same everyman connotation as "Tom, Dick, and Harry" in English) will provide her no satisfaction. It is a matter of the essential frigidity of the human animal, encased in his ego and unable fully to commit himself to love or selflessness. *Sodom and Gomorrah* describes the marital disillusion predicted in *Judith* and *Song of Songs*, and its portrayal shows it frightful and inevitable. Marriage is cosmically damned. Jean's and Lia's marriage fails, as does Jacques's and Ruth's, not through any individual disabilities, but by a failure of the species—a failure of man and woman, separate and rival races in God's creation.

This inevitable and fatalistic character of the marital holocaust has a deistic basis in *Sodom and Gomorrah*, which uses its biblical setting to blame the sexual crisis on the complicity of a monstrous, Old-Testament God. "I don't know why God hates me," says the gardener in the prologue, and neither the archangel nor the characters in the play can answer his question. The problem is that God himself does not know why. "He is like us. He doesn't understand," says Lia (II:5). It is a morbid and eerily nauseous determinism, where even God is buffeted by forces beyond his control. Never is man so helpless, in Giraudoux, as he is in this play. Never is he so despised of heaven, and never has heaven been drawn in a state of such chaotic ignorance and disorder.

The situation of the play is simply the inevitable failure of marriage and the consequent destruction of society; the action is little more than a few haphazard attempts to deal with the situation. Externally there is almost no action whatsoever, a feature which doubtless has contributed to *Sodom's* lack of stage popularity. Internally the action is structured on various disparate lines. The problem of adjusting to marriage is thrown on the shoulders of the several humans affected. "It was necessary for the angel to pose the problem. It is up to us to resolve it," says Lia (I:2). In the two long acts various solutions are proposed, then spurned. Then the world mercifully comes to an end.

Lia's "solution" is a wild attempt to seduce the angel of God. While this is a spiritual longing more than a physical one, it is not platonic; it is a sublime eroticism. Lia cries to the angel:

> I don't have to touch you. I no longer need my hands, my bosom, my lips—I don't need them because I am no longer in the shadow where I must crouch and beg. I stand in brightness. What do I want? I only beg for your light. [I:4]

It is a primal lust, generated by infantile memories, goaded on by a love for perfection, a lust for the "rays of light from your waist which have guided me from infancy" (I:4). But the angel is unreachable. The situation is the tragic dialectic: Jean and Jacques (humanity) are insufficient; the angel (destiny) is unavailable. Lia, trapped between possibilities, rejects a middle course:

Angel: Another will come.
Lia: Heaven doesn't yet understand women if it thinks I could possibly choose someone in the middle. It's you or him.
Angel: The angel or the beast?
Lia: Heaven has put the question. Me? I choose the angel. [I:4]

Delilah, who appears in the play not as an ally to Lia but as an opponent, takes the alternate route; she goes for the beast. Samson is, by her admission, "*la plus bête*" of the Sodomites, the stupidest and most bestial husband in the town. He is a model husband for the virago Delilah; "when she wants him to die, she will kill him herself" (II:4). Clearly this solution is no happier than Lia's; neither the angel nor the beast makes a satisfactory partner in a viable human relationship.

Jean's solution is a practical one; it is simply to put a mask of well-being over the fundamental discord. Jean sees himself as beyond the schism. He prefers the angel (considering the personality of his wife, this is hardly a surprise), but he is willing to forget about it, to lie about it.

Lia: You prefer the angel too, don't you?
Jean: I prefer the angel. I didn't have the gall to tell him, as you did, but I prefer the angel. [II: 5]

So Jean accepts the beast, hoping to find "a piece of the angel" in it. If he is disillusioned, he suppresses the fact. He works simply to project the appearance of well-being and happiness, unconcerned with the truth of that appearance. He buries himself in an image, behind verbal abstractions. He carves for himself a mask of the happy husband, one of a model couple. He tries to fool God. As Lia claims, "Oh my little Jean . . . life for you is a parade where couples file past arm in arm with their heads high. And if they are really pinching each other where no one can see, and smirking under those smiles, it's of no importance. It's only a matter of fooling God about his creatures . . . it's the mask of humanity for the eyes of their Creator" (I:3). And Jean agrees. Even at the moment of death he is obsessed with the idea of dying by his faithless wife's side, to show God that he was happy, to present to future generations a grotesque image of success. "That's what you want to be, what all men want to be: part of a family portrait," taunts Lia (II:8).

What is tragic in *Sodom and Gomorrah* is that Lia, bound to her origins as a *jeune fille*, unwilling to forgo that destiny which has been bred into her essential nature, refuses to buy Jean's solution. She rejects the mask. "I know your face and your mask," she tells him, "Many nights I passed my hand between your real and your false heart, your real and your false skin, your real and your false love. And I've tried to break through that abominable varnish. I shall have died in vain" (II:8). But she will not have stopped trying, and she will not forgo her savage assaults.

Jean has, of course, a more realistic point of view; so did the president in *Song of Songs*. Lia's insistence on absolute communion in love is unthinkable; two people ground together in a powder, literally, are two people who are dead. Jean cries in pain, "Poor Lia, you think you are tearing the mask off a human creature, but you are really tearing off his face" (II:8). But there is no appeasement to her implacability; one cannot quench an instinctive, primordial thirst with humanitarianism or rationality. Rationality is not at issue. Lia refuses even the final "family portrait"; as the world crumbles and burns, realizing in part her ultimate desire, she stands on one side of the city and he on the other. The men and women polarize about them. The desolation is Lia's final statement to God:

Jean: Lia, don't argue . . . come here next to me . . . as a woman next to a man.
Lia: No. If God sees all the women on one side embracing death, and the
    men on the other, he will understand. He didn't understand at the
    Deluge because he saw all those corpses of embraced couples floating
    about. [II:8]

Sodom and Gomorrah leaves a hollow ring; it is an empty signal to God. The final desolation is therapeutic, but the message does not get through to the heavens; unlike *Song of Songs*, the celebration of human tragedy goes unheard:

Jean: Heaven has ordered us to recite to it. In this moment of crisis and
    clarity it wants the Song of Songs of the false couple.
Ruth: Heaven's not listening. [II:2]

The final action is pointless: God doesn't care and the universe is breaking down. "Spare us the liturgy of the parting," says Lia (I:3), who recognizes all. The battering of primal lust against man's self-isolation enforces a queasy, unpleasant equilibrium of torments. *Sodom and Gomorrah* takes place in an empty universe, where, unique in the plays of Giraudoux, even language cannot gain a foothold. The dialectic is never so dumbly relentless as in the play's final moments:

    (*The end of the world. All is crumbled. The groups of men and women are
    nothing more than piles of cinders*)
Jean's voice: Forgive me, heaven! What a night!
Lia: Thank you, heaven! What a dawn!
Archangel: Won't they ever shut up! Won't they ever die!
Angel: They are dead.
Archangel: Then who's speaking?
Angel: They are. Death was not enough. The scene continues.
    (*The world disappears. The curtain falls*). [II:8]

Criticism awaits a definitive biography of Giraudoux which will "explain" the connections between this play and his own marital affairs (which, at least by French standards, seem to have been entirely normal).[12] But it is important to point out that *Sodom and Gomorrah* needs in no way reflect a particular domestic crisis in the author's personal life. The statement of Inskip, that "the play certainly bears testimony to his passage through moments of unbelief and lack of confidence unlike any hinted at in his previous work,"[13] mistakes the tone of the play for its action; for while *Sodom and Gomorrah* is rather lacking in the Giralducien wit, one finds the destruction of Sodom hardly dissimilar to the destructions of Troy and Argos in earlier plays; and the ugliness of mundane existence, in the presence of a malign, vindictive God, has been explored in all of Giraudoux's plays since *Judith*. *Sodom and Gomorrah* merely fulfills the prediction of *Judith* and *Song of Songs*, that "young girls are made for monsters, beautiful and hideous, but they are given to men. From then on, their lives are wrecked" (*Judith* II: 7). But it fulfills it with unusual passion. The bleak tone of the play is caused, most simply, by its subject: it is the first play that centers directly on human marriage. The play's conclusions about marriage are hardly different than Andromache's in *The Trojan War* (1935): "The life of a married couple who love one another is a perpetual, cold blooded waste. The dowry of true couples is the same as that of false ones: original discord" (*The Trojan War*, II: 8). But while Andromache's comments were virtually buried in the vast political panorama of *The Trojan War*, they become the central subject of *Sodom and Gomorrah*. Giraudoux's feelings on marriage had not changed, nor had his vision of a helter-skelter universe, where the Gods—both Greek and Hebraic—are as ignorant and malicious as the people they push around. What was different was the focus of the play, and the importance of the sexual conflict rather than the political one.

It must also be kept in mind that marriage, in *Sodom and Gomorrah*, has a symbolic rather than a literal meaning; it represents a specific form of man's adjustment to the world of human institutions. Lia is not simply a symbol of woman; she is a symbol of the human animal, nurtured with a love for the ideal, the spiritual, the "angel," and forced

---

[12] Giraudoux read all of his manuscripts to Suzanne, his wife, with the exception of this one. She guessed it was "because there were too many things about us in it. It is about the eternal problem of the misunderstandings between two beings who love each other and make each other suffer. . . . Yes, Jean loved to irritate me, to torment me. It never lasted long, of course, and soon he would come back more affectionate than ever. But he would disappear for weeks. Where was he? What was he doing? Imagine my feelings!" (In André Bourin, "Elle et lui: chez Madame Jean Giraudoux.") It is interesting that Giraudoux used his own name for his male protagonist in this play.

[13] Donald Inskip, *Jean Giraudoux: The Making of a Dramatist*, p. 128.

at one time or another to accommodate herself with a lying, face-saving "world of humanity." Like Judith and Florence, her forbears, she is simply a protagonist in the run of life; we follow her on the irreversible human treadmill which leads to the ultimate dryness: the death of ideals, the death of passion, and the death of the spirit. What makes Lia different from the others, and from ourselves, is that Lia must stop and rebel. She jams the machinery, and ends up by destroying the world. In a last attempt to communicate God's failure to God, she brandishes a flaming signal of martyrdom, but it is in vain; the treadmill simply continues.

Sodom and Gomorrah is a rough version of existentialist tragedy, where man is caught in the grip of an undefined, uncaring, unknowable world. All human contact has ceased. With telling prophecy of an entire body of drama to be based on this "lack of communication," Giraudoux writes:

Angel: Go away. No human has ever touched an angel.
Lia: Nor a human for that matter. But there's a great deal left to be said
　　about that.... [I:4]

In the world of Sodom, man (Lia) is left isolated in his own despair, able to count only his wasted destinies, his broken dreams, and his failure to preserve his ideals. The response is violent; an open, fiery, heedless rebellion. Lia, in bringing the destruction of the world about her ears, does so only for the bang—a giant last laugh in God's face. It is an existentialist response, an arbitrary seizure of destiny defined purely by volume, not direction. It is an absurd negativism. Even the apocalypse is meaningless.

The final catastrophe of *Sodom and Gomorrah* is God-ordained. Lia allows it, but she does not cause it or even choose it. She is not an existentialist heroine, ultimately, because it is her inaction rather than her actual will that brings on the disaster and determines the fate of Sodomite civilization. She, like the others about her, is a victim of forces—her plan is never positive, never more than a compulsive and ideological refusal to accept the plans of others. She hints darkly at an active plan, but never says what it is:

Ruth: We could abandon them? How about killing them?
Lia: There is also the third solution. [I:1]

We do not find out what this "third solution" is in *Sodom and Gomorrah*, but *Sodom and Gomorrah* was not Giraudoux's last word on the subject. Even as it was playing in Paris, Giraudoux was finishing his final play, *For Lucretia*. Although this play was not presented until 1953, it is the close sequel to *Sodom and Gomorrah*, and the final play of the sexual tetralogy. *For Lucretia* postulates the alternative ending to the problems of marriage (and by analogy, the problem of accommodation to the world of humanity): the alternative of suicide. It shows the sexual conflict taken to its ultimate conclusion.

For Lucretia

For Lucretia[14] was left in the collection of Giraudoux's manuscripts at the time of his death in January, 1944. It is a completed play but not a properly finished one, and the confusion of the manuscripts prevented an early premiere. The task of selecting a final copy fell to the director, Jean-Louis Barrault, who found a great variety of unordered and undated versions—two complete first acts, three complete third acts, and four complete versions of the final monologue, all ending with the author's handwritten stage direction, "the curtain falls."[15] Barrault was aided in his choice by earlier remarks of the late Jouvet, who had selected the same "final" version before his death, and this lent a further authenticity to the manuscript which was eventually produced and published. Despite the existence of alternative versions, however, the rendition which is now available is assuredly reliable. The variations from version to version are basically structural; the characters, plot, and style are generally consistent from one to the other. When we speak of *For Lucretia*, we are speaking of a complete Giraudoux play, and one of his most brutally honest.

The story of Lucretia, the virtuous Roman housewife, is known "to everyone who towards their tenth year had translated *De Viris Illustribus*,"[16] according to a French critic, who can take for granted the rigorous nature of a classical French education. The English world knows the story from Shakespeare's poem, a fairly traditional retelling.

---

[14] *Pour Lucrèce*. Christopher Fry has translated the play with the title *Duel of Angels*, perhaps taken from the Giraudoux novel, *Combat avec l'Ange*.

[15] Barrault, "À la Recherche de *Pour Lucrèce*."

[16] Léon Chancerel, "*Le Drame et le personnage de Lucrèce*," p. 55.

Lucretia, wife of Collatinus, is raped in the dead of night by the lusty prince, Sextus Tarquinus. Calling her husband and his friends around her, she stabs herself in humiliation. With the same dagger, drawn from her bleeding side, the brutal Tarquins are vanquished, the Empire is destroyed, and the Roman Republic is founded. The tale is simple and pathetic, well laden with melodrama and pagan moral heroism. But Giraudoux's version, not surprisingly, takes no more than the vaguest outline of the original.

Giraudoux gives the Roman legend a totally new locale, setting his drama in nineteenth-century southern France; specifically in the former Roman enclave of Aix-en-Provence in 1868. This was the period known in France as the Liberal Empire, when the power of Napoleon III was challenged by the Republicans. As Barrault notes, "Aix is not Rome, but it is Roman; Napoleon III is not the Roman Empire, but it is the Empire."[17] It was also, he might have noted, the last moments of Empire. Rome founded its Republic with Lucretia's bloody dagger, and France in 1868 was but two years from its Third Republic and the bloody Prussian War, which destroyed the French Empire once and for all. There is a *fin de siècle* mood about the play, which is reinforced by the quiet cry of despair over the lost heroism and the cowardice of a city under occupation in 1944. But it would be unwise to enlarge upon the relevance of the classical story or the political implications. The former is merely a form of literary nomenclature; an attempt to expand the story to archetypal importance by running it parallel to a distant legend; and the latter is the inescapable consciousness of a public servant who mourns, in *Sans Pouvoirs*, for his country, which, like Aix, is defeated but not bleeding. The true subjects of this play are the same as the last: human marriage and its partner, adultery. Giraudoux even suggests such a comparison with his prior play in the first scene, remarking that events have "advanced our gallant city of Aix to the level of Sodom or Gomorrah" (I: 1). *For Lucretia* is the final step of the sexual tetralogy, treating with compassion the culmination of human failure in the despair and suicide of the *jeune fille*.

The plot of *For Lucretia* is, for Giraudoux, quite complex. It follows the lines of the traditional love triangle, the basic stock of all French farce (and much French tragedy), and in Giraudoux's irrepressible manipulations, the triangle becomes pentagonal. To Aix, a city of love and lovers, comes Lionel Blanchard, the *procureur* (prosecuting attorney), and his wife Lucile. They have come from Limousin, Giraudoux's

[17] Barrault, "À la Recherche de *Pour Lucrèce*," 81–82.

native province, "the country which has given the world the most popes and the fewest lovers" (I:2), and their goal is to set a standard of absolute purity in the lackadaisical southern town. The judge denounces "Vice" from his judicial bench with the fury of an American Senate Committee chairman, singling out the local Don Juan, Count Marcellus, for special vilification. Lucile, who is at once the most beautiful and adored woman in Aix, loses her popularity as she stubbornly sits on *her* "bench" in the town's café and relentlessly denounces all traces of marital infidelity. She is a prosecutor of a more metaphysical order. "Wherever this *procureuse charmante* goes, life takes on the form and shape of the Last Judgment," says Marcellus (I:1); and Lucile's confidante accuses her: "you've returned original sin to the town . . . you've put the taste of Hell back into unconsciousness and innocence . . . you haven't come from Limousin, but from the Middle Ages" (I:2). Like the *jeune filles* who have come before her, Lucile combines absolute purity with utter implacability; she bears little resemblance to the kindly heroine of the Roman original. "Don't you think you're Lucretia," her confidante tells her, "You are the angel of evil" (I:2).

Lucile is an Electra let loose upon the world of domestic tranquility; Like Electra's, her drive to ferret out truth heeds no consequence. She has all the hallmarks of a creature of destiny: she is *la plus belle* in Aix and the woman most admired by the men. She is both angelic and pitiless (I:2), and her vision is superhumanly incisive: "Among the engagement rings and family jewels, you alone will detect the one that's false," says a friend (I:2). She can make others see that falsity as well, and when they do, they are condemned to live with it. The play's initiating action occurs when Lucile stubbornly betrays the lusty adulteress, Paola, to her husband, Armand. "Armand was the most gallant of peacocks, with a hundred blind eyes on his flourished tail. You have made those eyes see" (I:6). When destiny makes a man aware of the truth, he cannot pretend to ignore it. Aware of his wife's infidelity, Armand is forced to leave her.

Lucile's vision of love is antiseptic, noncorporeal. She is treated as a virgin in the play, for though she has been married five years, her husband is considered "your tutor, your uncle" by the sensual Paola (I:8). Lucile's psychological platonism is severe: "Flesh! You dare pronounce that horrible word in my presence. To say that I have flesh!" (III:3.)

Naturally, Paola is the exact opposite. "Pour moi," she says, "c'est le contraire" (I:8). The dialectic in the play is between the amorous promiscuity of Paola and the spiritual fidelity of Lucile: "Vice and virtue are going to contemplate each other face to face for the first time" (I:1). Paola is sexuality incarnate. She has twenty lovers and she loves each of them completely—in their presence, not at all in their absence. She mocks Lucile's idealized vision of love with a paean to physicality:

Paola: (mimicking) "You are near to me in your absence!"—Liar! Absence is absence, that is to say—death. When the one I love is going to leave me, for a day, even for an hour, I kneel at his feet, I cry, I moan, I hide his shoes, I beat myself in a gamble to start a fight, to keep him, not to lose him, not to lose *life*. . . . If you loved a man you wouldn't run off smiling toward your raspberry ice cream. You would lie down dead on a bed of plunder. [I:8]

Though opposites, Paola and Lucile are forcibly joined in an unholy alliance, the dialectic of carnality and spirituality. Together they ally to define woman from the time of Eve:

Paola: My sister, Lucile!
Lucile: Never! I will never be one of yours. Your devilish tricks can do nothing. Nor can your serpent's hissing.
Paola: (slowly, taking pleasure in hissing her words) Yessss, yesssss. [II:5]

Where Lia, in the previous play, combined her lust for carnal and spiritual satisfactions, these aspects are divided, in *For Lucretia*, between the two women. It is a structural improvement over *Sodom and Gomorrah* since it permits a genuine dialogue. "We have found each other again, face to face as on the ledge of a glacier," says Paola (III:4), and the bulk of the play is the forced dialectic between these two points of view, resulting, perhaps, in a melodramatic story, and yet a definition of the human animal which must stand as Giraudoux's final word on the subject.

Paola's vengeance on Lucile is wicked: she drugs her and leads her to the bedroom of Marcellus, where the town bloodletter, Barbette, persuades Lucile that she has been raped by the amorous count and, worse, that she has enjoyed it. Lucile goes to Marcellus and begs him to take his own life, whereupon he actually attempts to seduce her. Armand faithfully defends Lucile by killing Marcellus in a duel, but her scandalized husband walks out on her, forcing her to realize that his virtue is no deeper than his robes of justice. The behavior of the Aixois is despicable and dishonest. Even Lucile finds she is falling into an adulterous love with Armand. "Humanity is humanity," shrugs the decent Armand, "humanity is promiscuous" (I:7). Lucile's illusions, one by one, are shattered. While she has conceived her duty as awakening men to the truth, it is her own awakening that is described in *For Lucretia*.

The awakening is pathetic. "O Death! O Death!" Lucile vainly cries as Marcellus roughly describes her body to her. "It isn't by the mouth nor by the brains that a woman's truth, her confession, is pulled from her: it's by the entrails" (II:2), he tells her, and she feels strangely dejected when she at last finds out that her "rape" was imagined. The onrush of events shows reality more clearly, without the varnish of illusion. "It's very rare, in time of catastrophes, for misfortune to have the time to provide us with the usual masks," Armand tells her (III:3). Lucile sees the townspeople about her, including her hypocritical husband, with greater insight, and it disgusts her. She pleads with Armand to let her know what a man is truly like and receives this disillusioning response:

Armand: He is naïveté and illusion. He thinks at first that the world belongs to him, from top to bottom, and I'm speaking of a modest man. He then thinks that at least his wife belongs to him, that love belongs to him, and I'm speaking of an intelligent man. Then his hopes of life are replaced by the "joys" of life; he groans silently all through the night, and cries, but with dry eyes.

The word "dry" is part of the Giraudoux code; it describes Judith's capitulation to the rabbis and Florence's to marriage. The conflict between dry worlds of humanity and wetter ones of destiny is the subject of *Ondine*, which clearly speaks of mislaid destinies, broken dreams, defeated hopes, all accompanied by the acceptance of dry, mundane "joys" of domestic life.

But Lucile takes a step unlike any other Giraudoux heroine; although her disillusionment with life is total, she neither gives in to humanity nor permits its destruction. Lucile becomes the only Giraudoux heroine to take her destiny into her own hands, and by her act, momentarily to reverse its perpetual motion. The scene is operatic:

Lucile: I beg your pardon!
Paola: Is she mad? Pardon for what?
Lucile: For having said that life was unworthy and impure!
Paola: But isn't it? Have you found it worthy today?
Lucile: It is hideous. It is utterly debased, utterly absurd. I see wretched vermin crawling and gnawing each other on earth. It is the human race.

Paola: And is it pure? This man here, someone else's husband, you love him
  don't you?
Lucile: Yes, I love him. I hate my husband. But that man who yesterday
  was in your arms, I love him.
Paola: Then we agree completely, Lucile! Life is a defeat, my poor friend,
  and there's no recourse.
Lucile: No recourse? How wrong you are! Here it is, in my hand, my
  recourse! [III:6]

And Lucile takes a vial of poison that she stole from her husband
earlier in the play. She drinks it. The recourse, the poison, is her victory
over life. It is, in a metaphorical sense, her destiny—her self-identity
as a *jeune fille*.

Lucile: I look upon it as a little girl, who had my name, my age, and who
  had sworn, when she was ten years old, never to admit evil into her
  life; who had sworn to prove by her own death if necessary, that the
  world was noble and that human beings were pure. This earth has
  become empty and vile for her, this life nothing more than a forfeit;
  unimportant, untrue. She is keeping her oath! [III:6]

It is the supreme, self-willed repudiation of life, an existential suicide.
Death is the only way of stilling destiny, of quieting man's fruitless
desires to know, to interpenetrate another human being in love, to find
the apocalyptic sexual experience. And suicide is the only positive cure
for the human "disease" of warring truths; the divorce between destiny and human reality. Lucile's suicide is not a retreat, it is a momentary
welding of these worlds:

Lucile: I have won. The world is pure, Paola, the world is full of beauty
  and light. Tell me that yourself. I want to hear it from your lips. Tell
  me quickly.
Paola: . . . It is. For one second.
Lucile: That's enough. That's more than necessary. [III:6]

And Lucile dies happily.

It should be clear that Giraudoux does not advocate suicide in *For
Lucretia* any more than Ibsen does in *Hedda Gabler*. The drama is metaphorical, and Lucile is obviously an exceptional being. Her situation is
symbolic, a portrayal of the final transition of the *jeune fille* into an
awareness of the mendacity of human nature and the faithlessness of
man. Life is a defeat, perhaps, but the defeat can be accepted or rejected. The "normal" human being takes it. He is not beset by philosophical or ethical problems; his difficulty reconciling his childhood

dreams to his adult reality is a problem ameliorated with the moderate entertainments of life, and the appeasements of alcohol, television, and sporting events. But the defeat remains, and expresses itself in tiredness. Giraudoux wrote:

For most men, their trade generally clashes with their life, their spiritual existence. For women, their occupations and even their leisure activities seldom follow their tastes and preferences. Human existence is hardly anything but fatigue, and the constant job of adjustment which makes man daily, even hourly, modify his life in respect to others and to various circumstances. We are often tired at night from not having had, from rising to sleeping, that unity of heart, of morals, of occupation, or of joys which is the privilege of the nonhuman creatures. We die tired, in the evening of our life, from that awful tearing apart, that attempt at adjustment which in the end has been so completely in vain.[18]

Lucile, in rejecting life, rejects the tiredness born of continual compromise. She rejects the "tearing apart" of the forces about her, humanity and destiny, and she calls a momentary halt to the relentless dialectic. Her solution, suicide, is thematically the perfect ending for this play, and for the sexual tetralogy as a whole. It is the only valid climax to the discussion, which otherwise would continue forever (as it does in *Sodom and Gomorrah*) since each side is "right." Suicide, once considered clumsy dramaturgy, is structurally implicit in existential and absurdist drama, and is used with increasing frequency in contemporary plays.[19] It is an honest theatrical response to the existential dilemma.

Though she is perhaps unpleasant and unlikable, Lucile stands for something quite necessary in human affairs. As Barbette says, "Purity is not for this world, but every ten years there is a ray of it, a brilliant light. Under that light of purity, mankind sees itself as an ignominious merry-go-round" (III:7). Wedded to amorousness and hypocrisy, mankind needs the vision of the obstinately pure, the spiritual, the childish, the insane. Lucile, like Electra, Judith, Agatha, Aurélie, and Lia, is a madwoman. "*Elle est folle?*" says Paola (III:6); "*Vous êtes*

---

[18] Giraudoux, *Les Cinq Tentations de La Fontaine*, in his *Œuvres littéraires diverses*, p. 323.

[19] There are still few on-stage suicides like Lucile's (Jerry's in *Zoo Story* is one). But there are implicit suicides (or self-allowed immolations) as the final action in a great many contemporary plays: *The Visit, The Lesson, The Chairs, Death of a Salesman, Tiny Alice, A Man for All Seasons, The Maids*, etc. This is a recent development. William Archer, in 1912, explained to budding playwrights that what they had "chiefly to guard against is the temptation to overdo suicide as a means of cutting the dramatic knot. . . . It is . . . such a crude and unreasoning means of exit from the tangle of existence that a playwright of delicate instincts will certainly employ it only under the strongest compulsion." (*Playmaking, A Manual of Craftsmanship*, Boston, 1912, pp. 357–58).

folle," says Lionel Blanchard (III:2). In a time of vice and corruption such as existed in prewar and wartime Paris, a mad, insistent voice is necessary to redress the balance of compromise. "Thanks to her the pitch of our town has been elevated. Aix was lacking in grandeur and heroism," says Armand (II:3). In the life of the human, the reminder of his destiny and his ideals must never be too deeply suppressed. In her beauty, her grace, her noble Limousin heritage, her associations with purity and destiny, one can even see a little of Giraudoux himself.

The dialectic is as strong as a steel alloy. Life is composed of equal opposites: Destiny and Humanity, Vice and Virtue, Spirituality and Corporeality. Disillusion may be the natural state of man, but it is a dynamic state—a continual pulling from an ideal world versus the oppression of an existing one. The rare flashes of destiny in man's life are rarely benign: they cause social and personal annihilations, and in extreme cases leave in their wake corpses—and Pentateuchs. But the forces of humanity are no less powerful. Paola, as well as Lucile, is implacable; she too has gone through the transitions of life from *jeune fille* to adulterous *femme*, and she shares the power and the sexual desires of Judith and Lia—Judith who wishes "to be plundered," and Lia who seeks the absolute sexual and spiritual commingling of souls. Interestingly, the continuity of the tetralogy was preserved in the original production of *For Lucretia*, in which Lucile was played by Madeleine Rénaud, the original Florence, and Paola by Edwige Feuillère, the original Lia. Both characters are *jeunes filles* at different stages of life. Lucile simply chooses not to go on.

That *For Lucretia* is an honest play, thematically, has not made it a great one, however. The action is conventional and melodramatic, a problem that Giradoux capitalizes on at times but never overcomes. Thus such explanations as "Intermission for the drama, Lucile, it's time for bourgeois comedy" (II:5), or "You are in a melodrama and I am in real life" (II:4) or "Both of you are hunting for tragedy, but you're up to your necks in farce" (III:4), among many theatrical allusions, do little to persuade us that the form is independently interesting. Admitting a defect does not necessarily make it more acceptable, and Giraudoux was obviously uncomfortable in the realistic, melodramatic medium.

Moreover, the problems of the sexual tetralogy are graver than this. The successful production of any of the four is almost unheard of.[20]

---

[20] With the exception again of the Rabb-Harris *Judith* in New York.

For Lucretia, despite an excellent cast in its premiere and an equally celebrated cast in its English and American premieres (in Fry's translation), has never drawn an appreciable audience. The other three plays have done much worse. *Song of Songs*, though it may linger in the repertoire of the *Comédie Française*, is "beyond all doubt the least successful of all Giraudoux's writings for the theatre," according to a biographer-critic,[21] and *Sodom and Gomorrah* challenges it for unpopularity. *Judith* was Giraudoux's first failure, and its reception was disastrous. Benjamin Crémieux, a critic and friend of the author, wrote: "the interest of the spectator . . . cannot be profoundly moved, either by the story or by the heroine."[22] Gaston Rageot suggested that Giraudoux had fallen into the novelist's trap: "It seems that we have found nothing in this play of the author of *Siegfried*, and that we have been led back to the game of ideas and images which has enchanted the novelist and his readers. . . . The idea of the play is a pretty one, entirely true, unfortunately it has not been translated into drama . . . the action defeats itself."[23] François Porché, in the *Revue de Paris*, suggested that "Giraudoux the man of the theatre was swallowed up by Giraudoux the man of letters,"[24] a charge which Giraudoux bitterly resented and even attempted to answer.[25] But the charge was truthful enough, and it applies to all the sexual plays. Robert Mérac, writing in *Gringoire* of *Song of Songs*, kindly remarked: "It is a very pretty text which ravished me in the hearing, but which I will reread with a pleasure subtler yet";[26] and the critics of *Sodom and Gomorrah* and *For Lucretia*, while they upheld the beauty of the plays as literature, attacked the dramaturgy. Though vibrantly alive intellectually, and solidly honest in their expression of human dichotomies, they are poorly conceived for the theater.

Truth, though it may be a criterion for a good play, has never been a valid excuse for a dull one. Giraudoux's art as a dramatist lay in his ability to exploit the human dilemma, not simply to explain it. The sexual tetralogy, with its emphasis on realism and psychological probing, was an uneasy milieu for his imaginative talents, and he proved

[21] Donald Inskip, *Jean Giraudoux*, p. 96.
[22] *La Nouvelle Revue Française*, 37 (December 1931): 974.
[23] "Giraudoux Redevient Giraudoux," *Revue Bleue* (November 21, 1931), p. 706.
[24] Georges May, "Jean Giraudoux," p. 90.
[25] "Discours sur le théâtre," delivered at Chateauroux in 1931 and published in *Littéraure* (Paris 1941), pp. 231–41. Discussed below.
[26] "*Cantique des Cantiques* à la Comédie Française," *La Petite Illustration*, no. 899 (December 17, 1938).

unable to invest the characters with the facets which could allow them to rest comfortably at the center of such important discussions. It is not the lack of depth that we feel in these plays, but the lack of breadth. The uneasily narrow focus on the affairs of one or two individuals required a more detailed character analysis than Giraudoux desired, or was able, to give. His sexual dramas are peopled with characters whose sexuality is only indicated, never actually flowering. Only the most subtextually sensual of performances can bring Judith, or Lia, or Paola to life. The abilities of Giraudoux were not up to the task of creating a fully-fleshed, Chekhovian character, yet this is the structural demand of the sexual plays, where a philosophy of life depends upon the affairs of an individual in crisis. The reality of the philosophy depends on the reality of the crisis and the reality of the individual. Both are lacking in Giraudoux's honest but overtheoretical creations.

A second difficulty in the sexual plays is their failure to elicit empathy for the protagonist. The reason is simply that the heroines of the sexual plays are caught in an inexorable dialectic of which they are only scantly aware. There is no effective choice between worlds, there are not even illusory choices. There is only the choice to accept life or to refuse it. The dilemma of the sexual plays is an irresolution strictly within the soul, a laceration between childhood idealism and the adult world. In the broader metaphysical and political plays, Giraudoux was to paint man as a constant in a world without footholds; this has definite theatrical advantages. In the sexual plays, it is man himself who is undefined, he himself who is his own enemy. This plays havoc with an audience. They want to support the underdog and see the villain trounced; Giraudoux gives them both personae in the same character. Truthful as the dialectic may be, it is dramatically uninteresting. The audience cannot support one Judith against the other, and they are bored.

The sexual dramas are dramas of classification. This means inaction. The final question of *Judith* is simply whether Judith is a heroine or a whore. One may well ask, Who cares? However brilliantly pursued, the problem of the play is finding the proper label for an offstage event. Almost nothing hinges on the selection of one label over another, and the end result, in any case, is that both labels are correct. There is no grasping, in the sexual plays, for anything but words.

Eugénie: Names have nothing to do with this story.
Lucile: For me they have a lot to do with it. [I:6]

And Lucile dies to have Paola *say* that the world is pure. *Sodom and Gomorrah* is also reduced to semantics:

Jean: All was lost at your first word.
Lia: My first word was: I love you. [II:8]

And Lia dies in search of a reality which matches the purity of that word.

The sexual tetralogy is a continuous history of human life, an etiology of the human disease. It traces a spiritual descent from the innocence of the young girl to the corruption of the wife/adulteress/suicide. The tetralogy is at the heart of Giraudoux's personal philosophy, and one is pleased that he could get it out of his system. The plays are brave attempts to enter the fields of psychology, motivation, and sexual aberration, which had formerly been the exclusive property of the naturalists. If they are failures as works of the theater, they are glittering failures; marvelous, brittle introspections of what it means to live on the human planet, and what it means to grow old. Without the substance of the sexual plays as a key, we would be harder pressed to understand the seriousness and the profundity of *Ondine* and *Intermezzo*, or *Electra* and *The Madwoman of Chaillot*. We shall find that the metaphysical and political plays are simply grand expansions of the direct, narrow themes of the sexual tetralogy. The metaphysical plays, particularly, are basically theatricalizations of the sexual ones. In enlarging his palette, in opening up a new and beautiful world of fantasy to express human destiny, Giraudoux combined structure, philosophy, and form into his most powerful set of plays, and the ones which will probably be his most lasting.

Two

THE METAPHYSICAL PLAYS

All of Giraudoux's plays are metaphysical or fantastic to some extent. *Judith* and *Sodom and Gomorrah* are peopled with roving angels, *Song of Songs* features a Spirit of Jewelry, *The Madwoman of Chaillot* includes the spirits of animals, vegetables, and "the Adolphe Bertauts of the world," and both *Electra* and *The Trojan War* involve the interventions of Greek deities. Nonetheless these plays are metaphysical mainly in their overtones. The truly metaphysical plays have fantasy imbedded in their architecture. The metaphysical plays concern the love affairs between humans and spirits.

René Marill suggests that Giraudoux uses Gods as "anthropomorphic images of destiny."[1] This is correct, yet its implications have not generally been realized. It is important to see that Giraudoux does not write "about the gods." Dramatically speaking, Giraudoux is an atheist. When Lia tries to make love to Sodom's angel, Giraudoux is not postulating an Old Testament cosmos any more than in *The Trojan War* he is postulating a Homeric one. In both cases the nomenclature of destiny has simply been borrowed from an earlier source. Lia's angel is nothing but a theatrical realization of Lia's lust. The metaphysical plays are not about Gods but about men, and fantasy is Giraudoux's expression of man's inward dreams.

Fantasy, for Giraudoux, was a liberating force. It allowed for an expansion of his philosophical concerns, a dramatic exploitation that was missing from the introspective, sexual plays. Of course this had commercial advantages in the theater, and Jouvet spared little expense to make Giraudoux's fantasy come brilliantly alive on stage. But the bedrock reality of Giralducien fantasy must be underscored. Fantasy is the perfect medium for the realization of dialectical premises.

[1] René Marill (Albérès) *Esthétique et morale chez Jean Giraudoux*, p. 360.

Giraudoux, writing in its liberated vocabulary, could embody truth, justice, and love in characters who were not held back by human frailties or dichotomies. As a result, the spirituality of Ondine, a fish, is less offensive and more appealing than that of Lucile, a woman. Giraudoux's fantasy is an exquisite mirage of the human unconscious.

The form of the fantasies is traditional: the eternal triangle. All of the metaphysical plays are romances. This was almost the case in *Sodom and Gomorrah*, where Lia offers herself to an angel. But in *Sodom and Gomorrah* the angel refuses. In the metaphysical plays he accepts. This is the leap into fantasy and intrigue. But the basic difference between Giraudoux and more conventional dramatists is that, in his eternal triangle, one point is on a different plane. This can probably be best shown through a diagram, thus:

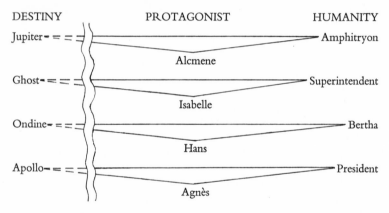

DESTINY   PROTAGONIST   HUMANITY

Jupiter — Amphitryon / Alcmene

Ghost — Superintendent / Isabelle

Ondine — Bertha / Hans

Apollo — President / Agnès

To the right of the line is the race of humanity in all its shades of erectness; to the left, and in the nether plane, the characters of fantasy and destiny. Man, torn in twain, is the helpless caryatid at the bottom.

The diagrams are oversimple, but that is the nature of the metaphysical plays. Purity may not exist in *this* world, as Babette says at the close of *For Lucretia*, but it is not denied to the fantasist. The Ghost is a ghost, Ondine is a mermaid, and Jupiter is the King of the Gods; characters of destiny need exhibit none of the dialectical imbalance which plagued the neurotic characters in the sexual plays. The dramatic benefit is obvious. Though the tragic theme is no less potent, the purity of fantastic expression lends a sublime theatricalization which is at the heart of Giraudoux's intention.

Amphitryon 38

Amphitryon 38 is the first of the metaphysical plays, and the chronological successor to the political *Siegfried*. It was the first of Giraudoux's plays to gain an appreciable international audience. The appeal of the play is its frankly libertarian humor and gaiety, factors which guaranteed its success in New York despite (or because of) a heavily cut English version by S. N. Behrman. It is one of the two plays that Giraudoux designated as "comedies" (the other being *Intermezzo*), and it fulfills that genre with elegance.

The title indicates that this is the thirty-eighth variation on the theme of Jupiter's rape of Alcmene, Amphitryon's virtuous wife; a "fact" which has no known documentation but adds a whimsical note of fatality to the tale. As Jupiter says, "It is not a question of knowing *if* I will have Alcmene, but *how*!" (III:4). A backlog of thirty-seven versions, Giraudoux implies, freezes his rendition of the story to the basic original outline: the sexual alliance between a beautiful woman and the king of gods, resulting in the birth of a demigod son, Hercules. Giraudoux follows this outline to the letter, and his treatment is a comic, frequently precious analysis of the forces of destiny at work on humanity.

This was Giraudoux's first reworking of a classical story, and while it is hardly the first French example of the genre, it spurred a tremendous revival of "modernized" Greek tales. Since the Renaissance, the French seem to have adopted the Greek legends as their own ancient history, and Giraudoux once told an interviewer, "The French spirit and the Greek are on the same plane. . . . Greek thought is French thought once the shell is broken."[2] Contemporary theater abounds with French revisions of Greek tales, but *Amphitryon 38* is one of the rare comedies so written. Most are tragedies (Anouilh's *Antigone*) or parodies (Cocteau's *The Infernal Machine*). The advantage of the form is that the plot is assured; the playwright simply delimits his occupation to detailing motivations and expressing philosophies; in fact this has become a very simple way to write "philosophical" plays (Sartre's

---

[2] André Rousseaux, "Un quart d'heure avec Jean Giraudoux," p. 3.

The Flies is an example), since the playwright need only interpret an existing play according to a given set of ideas or prejudices. Giraudoux went somewhat beyond this. Certainly the classical format allowed his intriguing speculations on the "true" motivations of, for example, warfare; and he did not shy from poking irreverent fun at the deities and demigods that are known from childhood. In addition, he accepted with obvious relish the mythological system of the Greeks, which, like his own, envisaged man on a fatalistic, God-driven course, helpless to alter his destiny by the force of will. But his principal use of the Greek system in *Amphitryon 38* was its provision of a world of destiny, ready-made. The Greek gods and goddesses are part of civilization's inherited mythic fantasy; they are accepted by tradition and have complete familiarity. Jupiter is immediately recognizable and iconographic. Moreover, he is colorful. The Greek gods have more theatrical personalities than the anonymous angels and archangels of *Sodom and Gomorrah*, and their paganism makes them far more harmonious with Giraudoux's amoral and nonreligious concept of destiny.

Amphitryon pits man between his fellows and the gods. Though a fantasy situation, it is one which has been used in the darkest of Greek tragedies. Typically, the situation is tragic and archetypal; the treatment gay and sparkling. The combination of a witty, comic text with a tragic subtext describes all the metaphysical plays and gives them their rare vibrations. "Out of all this tragedy of the gods, my dear Leda," says Alcmene, "let us make a little entertainment for women!" (II:6.) It is the basic Giralducien technique.

The intrusion of Jupiter into the faithful marriage of Amphitryon and Alcmene is an imposition of the absolute upon the human, the pure upon the dialectical. It is not a meeting of man and gods but a testament to the separation between them. Even conflict is impossible between these members of opposing worlds. Jupiter tells the stubbornly resisting Amphitryon, "This isn't even a real conflict when you come right down to it, it's only, alas, a conflict in form, like those which provoke church schisms and new religions" (III:4). Jupiter is the sovereign of the gods; Amphitryon is the inventor of window-pulleys. These characters cannot do one another battle; they merely demonstrate themselves. Alcmene has no effective choice between them. She may be faithful to Amphitryon but, like all *jeunes femmes*, she dreams of Jupiter.

The comedy is always in delicate balance with this predicament of separation. Jupiter spies on Alcmene and Amphitryon much as the gods hover over Lia and Jean in the later marital drama, and his divine demand is not for Alcmene's body but for her "consent" (I:1). It is apparent that Jupiter can do with her body as he wishes; already Mercury reports spying on her in her bath. But it is not rape that Jupiter desires, and he rejects Mercury's suggestion that he simply hoist her to a floating cloud for the divine act. He wants to conquer her will. He creates war between Amphitryon's Thebes and friendly Athens in order to drive Amphitryon out of town, then dresses as the absent husband and comes to Alcmene's bed. It is a clever ruse but it does not completely work. He gains her body but not her soul; Alcmene is no less faithful to her husband than before. Her will, like Lia's is adamant.

Alcmene and Amphitryon are a perfectly human couple. Their self-image is stalwartly honorable. She is "the most beautiful of the Greeks" (I:3), and he is a general in the army, a grafter of cherry trees, and an inventor of various devices for the home, somewhat like Jerome in *Song of Songs*. They play the game of love convincingly; Alcmene's first words to Amphitryon, and his to her, are identically pure: "I love you." Their love is properly physical, for as Amphitryon tells Alcmene, "presence is the only race of lovers" (III:3). And they consider themselves totally faithful to one another. Proudly Alcmene defends her fidelity: "People should stop speaking about fatality, it only exists because of the feebleness of mankind. The tricks of men, the desires of gods—these can do nothing against the will and the love of a faithful wife" (II:7). Alcmene's sentiments are noble. What she does not know is that she had been violated by Jupiter just hours ago, and is now in the process of sending her husband off to bed with another woman. The virtue of this couple is illusory. Fate remains inexorable; the human will can accept or reject it, but it goes on nonetheless. "Your union with Jupiter has been made since all eternity," says Mercury to Alcmene (II:5); it is a rendezvous with destiny which cannot be denied.

Mercury sees under the mask of human fidelity. He sees Alcmene from the inside. He sees her at her bath, and he sees her asleep; he knows her dreams.

Mercury: Faithful wives dream frequently, and dream that they are not in the arms of their husbands.

Alcmene: They are not in anybody's arms.

Mercury: It happens to these faithful wives that they call their husbands Jupiter. . . . Don't force me to speak crudely and show you what lies at the heart of what you consider candor. [II:5]

Faithfulness is a restraint, a compromise of the spirit to the demands of politic behavior. It is a suppression of the spirit, a sublimation of it; not a victory. "Faithful wives are those who look to the spring, to their reading, their perfumes, to the movements of the earth, for the revelations that other women demand from lovers. In sum, they are unfaithful to their husbands with the whole world—except with men. Alcmene is no exception" (I:5). This is a familiar theme, which Giraudoux continues with *Electra's* Agatha, who deceives her husband with the bedpost; and with Paola, for whom, as Lucile tells Armand, "there isn't a minute, there isn't a living being with which she does not perpetually deceive you" (*For Lucretia*, I:9). The conflict is between an inner and an outer fidelity; the faithfulness of the body versus the amoral infidelity of the heart. Giraudoux finds actual faithfulness nothing more than a human ritual, unallied with man's natural morality and easily betrayed in the unconscious freedom of his dreams. Jupiter argues that fidelity is contrary to love itself: "A wife's love becomes duty. Duty becomes constraint. Constraint kills desire" (I:6). Nothing in the play serves to contradict this statement.

Faithfulness is inimical to man's nature because of the thousands of contrary forces that continue to batter him. Faithfulness belongs to the pure: to gods and saints. Jupiter, assuming the form of a man for his conquest of Alcmene, falls prey to the human complexity:

Mercury: What do you actually want?
Jupiter: Oh God, what every man wants! A thousand contrary desires.
For her to be faithful to her husband and yet to give herself to me in all her ecstasy. For her to be chaste under my caresses yet for forbidden desires to burn in her as I watch her. [II:3]

Internal fidelity is strictly a matter for spirits, whose subconscious is organized on monolithic, simplistic lines. Man is not capable of such focus. He is captive to the human diseases: relentless change, aging, and pride. In the fantasy structure of *Amphitryon*, the world of the gods is a clear one; and world of man is "a terrible assortment of confusions and illusions" (II:2). The divine world is eternal, the world of man is crushingly mortal. "What I see right away, when I look at the living figure of a man, is that he is constantly aging. Right before my eyes I see his light dying" (I:5). But the irony of life is that man recognizes mortality only in others, never in himself. Jupiter, taking human shape, is given a mock interrogation by Mercury:

Mercury: Do you think that only you exist, that you are certain only of your own existence?

Jupiter: Yes. As a matter of fact, it's very strange to be imprisoned in
    myself like this.
Mercury: Do you have the idea that you are going to die someday?
Jupiter: No. My friends will die, yes, alas, they shall! But me? No ... for
    the first time I believe myself, I see myself, I feel myself truly a master
    of the gods.
Mercury: Then you are truly a man! [I:5]

Alcmene temporizes Jupiter's lust with her offer of "friendship,"
which, in its virginal purity, "couples the most unalike creatures and
makes them equal" (III:5). But her violation is a fait accompli. Although she senses that Jupiter has already made love to her and can do
so again whenever he wishes, she refuses him. Likewise Amphitryon,
admitting the futility of resisting him, resists him. At first glance the
futile resistance is heroic. But ultimately the resistance is against internal
forces; against self-knowledge and human understanding. Fidelity is
maintained only by a rigorous restraint. Jupiter offers Alcmene more
than a divine sexual experience. He offers her truth:

Jupiter: Alcmene, dear friend, I want you to participate, if only for a second,
    in the life of a god.... Wouldn't you like to see, in a brilliant flash,
    what the world is, and to understand it?
Alcmene: No, Jupiter, I am not curious.
Jupiter: Don't you want to see that void, that succession of voids, that
    infinity of voids which is eternity? ...
Alcmene: No.
Jupiter: ... Don't you want to see humanity at work, from its birth to its
    conclusion? Don't you want to see the eleven great beings that ornament
    its history, the one with the pretty Jewish face or the one with the
    little Lorraine nose?
Alcmene: No.
Jupiter: For the last time I ask you, obstinate woman! Don't you want to
    know, since you will soon forget everything anyway, which appearances
    constitute you happiness? Which illusions compose your virtue?
Alcmene: No. [III:5]

Alcmene prefers to keep her desires, the churning forces of her subconscious, hidden beneath that protective wall of human behavior
which covers over primordial reality and makes human life continue
with equanimity. She refuses knowledge and rejects the divine intrusion. Of course it is a futile rejection. The intrusion not only takes
place, it is celebrated in the cries of heavenly voices and the gamut of
mythic history. Much as Judith's avowals of guilt did nothing to as-
suage history's verdict of innocent, Alcmene's rejection of Jupiter is

forgotten by history's librettists. Her story is further rigidified by thirty-seven supposed dramatic precedents, and Giraudoux would never tamper with the end result of a tradition, no matter how much he might disfigure the paths to that result. What Alcmene chooses to believe about her surrender to Jupiter, and what Amphitryon chooses to believe about his cuckolding, is actually trivial in the cosmic scope of the play. The act alone counts. Its proof is in the child Hercules, the "cross between beauty and purity" (II:5), the demigod: half human and half god, epitomizing the union of two worlds, which only meet in fantasy. The act of divine intrusion in the affairs of man is affirmed.

Structurally, *Amphitryon 38* is a simple play which divides the world into two races and shows one member of each tending to move toward the other. As Alcmene discovers the attractions of the godly realm, so does Jupiter find himself captured by the human. In Giraudoux's fantasy, the neat pyramidal structure is complicated by dual protagonists, and while the principal triangle that describes the action of *Amphitryon 38* posits Alcmene at the apex, a subsidiary triangle describes Jupiter's *déchirement* between the world of humans and the heights of Olympus. At the risk of oversimplifying, the following diagram describes the tingling triangular alliances of the play:

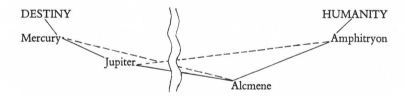

This same picture, with modifications and a change of cast, reappears for all the fantasy plays. It describes a permanent confrontation of the worlds, with the two protagonists attempting, and failing, to bridge the unbridgeable gap between them. Though the confrontation is permanent, it is not necessarily static. All characters are in flux and all move about incessantly trying to find the divine combination, which never comes.

The strengths of *Amphitryon 38* are not in the development of this structure, or in the dynamics of plot, but in the ceaseless vibrations of interplay between the human and godly worlds, the permeable and the absolute. The fantasy structure is a blanket excuse for what is otherwise considered a dramaturgic fault: superobjectivity. Giraudoux is free, in fantasy, to comment on the plight of man from the point of view of hypothetical gods. He is allowed, in other words, to define man externally, to contrast man's diverse behavior with the purity of supposed superhuman existence. Fantasy justifies this sort of witty epigram, which is rarely acceptable in serious drama: "To seduce [a woman] you must first please her, then undress her, then get her dressed again, then, in order to be able to leave her, displease her. It's a whole occupation in itself" (I: 1). In the mouth of a man this line would only qualify its speaker for farce. In the mouth of a god it enlivens without broadening the humor.

Amphitryon 38 has a gaiety altogether lacking in *Siegfried* and certainly missing from the other plays about marriage and its consequences. It is an ironic titillation of despair, not a complete submission to it. It is an overlook of the absurd without a complete commitment to it. The godly perspective is a safe retreat from the infectious mortality of mankind and its horrors. Gaiety, audiences from 1929 to the present have found, is a welcome approach to fatality.

Intermezzo

The gaiety is gone in *Intermezzo*,[3] but it is replaced by the warmth and delicacy of the human comedy. *Intermezzo* is one of Giraudoux's true masterpieces. As a combination of nostalgic humor, provincial beauty, and sophisticated, existential irony, it is his most perfect play. The metaphysical structure, unlike *Amphitryon 38*, is an original creation, more convincing and more pertinent than the iconographic Greek deities of *Amphitryon*. Originality is the hallmark of *Intermezzo*. It is the only play of Giraudoux's that has no source other than the author's fertile memory and imagination.

"Our town is mad," says one of the characters in *Intermezzo* (II: 1), and this becomes the basic predicament of the play: in the province of Limousin, an entire town has been suddenly transformed into that special madness which characterizes creatures of destiny. The town is in

---

[3] Known in English in Maurice Valency's translation with the title, *The Enchanted*.

a "poetic delirium" (II: 1), where the values of truth, justice, beauty, and magic have suddenly overruled the social structure of politeness, circumspection and adjustment. "Children whose parents beat them run away from home. Dogs whose masters ill-treat them bite their masters' hands. Women stuck to old, ugly, drunken, hairy husbands simply abandon them for sober, young, smoothskinned lovers" (I: 4). In the weekly lottery the cash prize is won by the town pauper for once, instead of the customary millionaire; and the motorcycle is taken by the town athlete instead of the mother superior. In the five-year census men list as wives, not their true spouses but the women they dream about, "even the female animal which represents for them the perfect companion, a cat or a squirrel" (I: 4). Clearly it is a wicked state of affairs for the proponents of Giralducien humanity. "An unknown influence is gradually undermining all the principles, albeit false ones, on which civilized society is based" (I: 4). An attack force is summoned. From Limoges, the capital of the province, comes the inspector to extirpate the cause of these disturbances. "Who am I?" he demands rhetorically, "I am humanity" (III: 1).

He finds the villagers convinced that the cause of the local madness is a ghost who has been hovering about the town since his supposed murder-suicide months ago. The inspector's investigation uncovers the fact that the ghost is being fed—"and perhaps with dessert" (II: 2)—by Isabelle, the town's substitute schoolmistress, who "is purity and honor itself" (I: 5). Isabelle is seizing upon a lifelong desire: to make an alliance with the dead, and to comprehend the secrets of the universe. It is the dream of all *jeunes filles*—to make contact with destiny. In this case destiny is a handsome ghost, a refuge from the world of the dead. The dead, from their greater-than-Olympian vantage, are all-comprehending and extraterrestrial; just the sort of idols for a *jeune fille* like Isabelle. *Intermezzo* is basically a play about death; an attempt to prove that, as Isabelle hopefully suggests, "the contradiction between life and death has only been created by human agitation" (III: 3). In trying to reconcile the dead with the living, Isabelle endangers society on the cosmic plane, but Isabelle, and *Intermezzo*, are removed to the "safe" form of fantasy, and the conflict is described with whimsy and theatricality.

The originality of the concept demanded more plotting than *Amphitryon 38*, since Giraudoux could not leisurely reexplore a familiar tale about familiar characters. The story is a romance. The townsmen, including the mayor, the druggist, and the handsome young superintendent of weights and measures, try to persuade Isabelle to give up her liaison with the ghost so that he will go away and leave the town in peace. The inspector prefers the use of force, and hires two hangmen to shoot the ghost; the act fails when the ghost of the ghost rises from the riddled corpse and continues his interference in the town's life. The superintendent's approach is more successful; he offers himself as an earthly rival to the ghost for Isabelle's favors. Explaining to her that life as the wife of a government *fonctionnaire* can be colorful and exciting too, he succeeds in drawing her away from her spiritual alliance. Isabelle's transition from *jeune fille* to *jeune femme*, however, is violent. As the ghost departs forever, Isabelle falls into an unearthly coma, into "disincarnation" (III:5). Only by the ingenious intervention of the druggist is she revived; he organizes the villagers into a "Fugue for the Provincial Chorus," an orchestrated collection of the everyday sounds of rural life, which finally succeeds in bringing her back to the human world. The village returns to normal: in the lottery the millionaire again wins the cash prize, and the motorcycle goes to the cripple at the orphanage. Isabelle can now marry the superintendent. "I have put your district back in order," declares the inspector (III:6). "The interlude is over," declares the druggist (III:6).

It has been quite an interlude, or *intermezzo*, at that. Aside from the comings and goings of such romantic and ridiculous characters, Giraudoux has provided a pair of scatterbrained virgin aunts, appropriately named Mangebois (eat wood), and Isabelle's students, the *fillettes*, who laugh riotously at everything the inspector says. The singing hangmen and the enterprising townspeople rival each other for decorativeness. But the theme of the play is of significance. What must not be overlooked, above all, is that if Giraudoux had allowed Isabelle to die in the final scene, the play could have been made into a tragedy with only the slightest revisions.

The internal framework is identical to that of *Amphitryon*, and the two plays present an interesting comparison for that reason—one being an adoption of a metaphysical system, the other being its creation. Isabelle, like Alcmene, is the eternal young girl torn between rivals who come from different worlds: The ghost (destiny) and the superintendent (humanity). These characters are drawn as typically as possible: the ghost is handsome, spiritual, and all-knowing. The superintendent is a *fonctionnaire*, ordinary, simple-minded, kind, and slightly absurd. Both characters are emissaries from their worlds, not absolute representations. As Jupiter is a god who comes down to earth, so the ghost is one of the dead whose affection for humanity still lingers. And the superintendent, though wedded to the life of humanity, is still sympathetic with the appeal of destiny. Giraudoux has completed the metaphysical framework by adding its extremities—the nameless dead on the left, and the inspector on the far right. Thus:

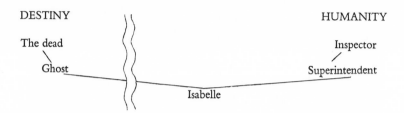

Other characters arrange themselves variously on the right (humanity) side of Isabelle, with the druggist separating himself from the graphic system as the wise old voice of Giraudoux himself. He is, in effect, the stage manager of the larger play: Life. "At my age, mademoiselle, each of us must come to an understanding of what character destiny has intended him to play on the stage of life. *I* am here to make transitions" (I:7). The transition of this play is Isabelle's; from *jeune fille*, the spiritual lover of ghosts and abstractions, to *jeune femme*, the young wife of the superintendent. It is a transition not unlike those of the heroines of the sexual plays, but the playwright's palette has broadened to include directly the cosmic transitions, which, in the bleaker plays, are only metaphorically implied.

Isabelle stands "on the very seam of the province" (II:3). She attempts, as do all Giraudoux protagonists, to reconcile the two worlds which vie for her membership. "*Intermezzo*", of course, means "in the middle," and this cosmic dichotomy is the implication of the title. Isabelle is battered one way and the other, and her final transition to humanity almost costs her her life. The two worlds can never touch; they are "in two completely different registers of life" (II:5). Isabelle tries to hold hands with both worlds, and for a moment she seems to succeed. But like all *jeune filles* she must convert. The "yank" of humanity is inescapable except by death, a final recourse which she actually requests ("save me from happiness...!" [III:4]), but is denied. The element of bitterness is not missing in Isabelle's fatal acceptance of the very human superintendent, "that being encased in cement," as the ghost refers to his fleshy rival (III:4). Before the ghost leaves as the twice-jilted lover, he relates, in a vital Giraudoux *tirade*, "the complete adventure of the *jeune fille*:"

> *Ghost:* This is the complete adventure of the *jeune fille*.... Seated in the fields, their parasols open beside them, leaning on railway crossings and waving goodbyes to passing travelers, or by a lamp behind their windows, with the street a shadow in front of them and their room a shadow behind them, like flowers in winter, they are skillfully scattered among the crowd of men, the generous one in the family of misers, the strong one in the family of cripples, so that the divinities of the world take them, not for humanity in its infancy, but for the supreme efflorescence, the ultimate result of a race whose true product is the elderly. But suddenly ...
> *Superintendent:* This is silly.
> *Ghost:* But suddenly man arrives. They all stop and look at him. He has found the ways to raise their eyes to appreciate their earthly dignity. He stands on his back paws, so as to receive less of the rain and to hang medals on his chest. They shiver before him with a hypocritical admiration, and a fear greater than even a tiger would instill in them, ignorant that only this biped, among all meat-eating animals, has teeth which rot. Then it's all over. All the windows into reality ... become opaque for them, and everything is finished.
> *Superintendent:* Finished? If you are alluding to marriage, don't you mean that it's just beginning?
> *Ghost:* And the pleasure of the nights begins. And the habit of pleasure. And gluttony begins. And jealousy ... and vengeance. And indifference begins. On the throat of man, the collar slackens. All is finished. [III:4]

This last line is perhaps the most ironic double entendre in Giraudoux. In French it reads, "*Sur la gorge des hommes, le seul collier perd son orient. Tout est fini.*" On the one hand this says that the necklace (*collier*) loses its lustre (*perd son orient*), or that life loses its appeal. But the more important meaning is that the collar (also *collier*) loses its lift (also *perd son orient*), and that the leash which has yanked us into the world of humanity is no longer needed to hold us up. Man is finally able to stand on his own. When that happens, of course, *tout est fini*. It is the grisly etiology of life, sex, and marriage, which is continued in a less "silly" vein in *Sodom and Gomorrah*. The imagery of man "standing on his back paws" as in his first appearance on earth, distinguished in his first moments from other mammals, is the literal image of man "yanked" to his feet and held there by pride (hanging medals on his chest) and practicality (remaining drier in the rain). Marriage, as foretold by Jupiter in *Amphitryon 38*, by the president in *Song of Songs* and by Armand in *For Lucretia* is a series of compromises which leads to spiritual debasement. Isabelle, younger and more curious than Alcmene, still wants to comprehend the universe, but her acceptance of humanity prevents this. The windows to reality, to sublime knowledge, close for her. Isabelle recoils in horror from a cruel future, but she must accept it:

Isabelle: Why this cruelty? Save me from this "happiness" . . .
Ghost: Adieu, Isabelle. The superintendent was right. What men love, what you love, is not to understand, not to know, it is to oscillate between two truths, or two lies . . . [III:4]

The oscillation is the dialectical torment of man trapped between two worlds.

Of course, the metaphysical-philosophical structure of *Intermezzo* is only a framework for a comic and touching play, and it is more clear than ever, in this work, that Giraudoux's ideas are basically subservient to the theatricality they engender. The structure of *Intermezzo* permits three areas of creative invention from the playwright: the evocation of a manufactured world of destiny, the parody of the world of humanity, and the gentle tenderness of a life which, by necessity, must be lived between them.

Destiny is characterized by its image, the absolute light of the sun. The behavior of the townspeople affected by the madness is merely "agreement with the sun" (I:4). Isabelle's schoolchildren are taught "The Marseillaise of little girls," which goes "*A Marseille, à Marseille, La patrie, c'est le soleil!*" (I:6.) The presence of absolute light in the affairs of the town brings about a natural, animalistic morality and overthrows social structures, including the basic tenets of Christian behavior. "Weakness is no longer a force, nor is affection a habit," explains the superintendent (I:4). "Bourgeois morality is at the moment ass-backward" says the Inspector a bit more crudely (I:5). In short, all behavior is instinctual and immediate, and no contracts, fiscal or marital, are upheld. Rather than teaching her students about codes of etiquette, Isabelle eulogizes the beauty of the human body, and has them vote on the handsomest man in town. She teaches them, not the difference between monocotyledons and dicotyledons but that "the tree is the immovable brother of man," and that "the right angle does not exist in nature. The closest to it is the angle described by an imaginary line from the Greek nose to the Greek soil" (I:6). "*Folles!*" cries the inspector (I:6).

Isabelle's "progressive" ideas of education, not very unlike experiments tried in America and Europe, are a reaction to the strict classical education which remains the norm in France. With irony she recalls her own education in the convent:

Isabelle: All we were taught, my comrades and I, was a civilization of egotists, a politeness of termites. Little girls, *jeunes filles*, we were supposed to lower our eyes before birds that were too brightly colored, clouds too sculptural, men too manly, and everything in nature which was a "sign." We left the convent knowing only the narrowest part of the universe—the inside of our own eyelids. [II:3]

This form of education she rejects for her students, understanding it to be a weapon against mankind, a tool for the suppression of natural desires.

Isabelle: What is called human understanding is actually the human religion, a terrible egoism. Its dogma is to make any liaison with the nonhuman world impossible, to sterilize it, to make man unlearn all languages, with the exception of the human, which a child already knows. [II:3]

Isabelle prefers to teach and to live by a mystical apperception of the spiritual world. She creates a nonhuman and nondeistic religion, governed by "The Unifier," who soothes the wounds of the human *déchirement*, and by "Arthur," a spirit who provokes mischief in the affairs of men. She chides Christians for pretending to believe in a life after death without actually believing it (II:3). She lives in a world of poetry and simple beauty, which Giraudoux stylistically portrays in her twilight meetings with the ghost. Only an author sensitive to the rhythm of dreams could write, as in the first exchange between Isabelle and her Ghost:

Isabelle: Je m'excuse, de cette tache de soleil!
Ghost: C'est passé. La lune est venue.
Isabelle: Vous entendez ce que disent les vivants, tous les vivants?
Ghost: Je vous entends.
Isabelle: Tant mieux. . . .

The world of humanity is drawn with Giraudoux's cleverest satire; indeed, the presence of the inspector in *Intermezzo* gives the play a needed comic freedom. The inspector is a gross exaggeration of human needs, as much a creature of fantasy as the ghost. "Humanity is a superhuman enterprise," he declares (III:1), betraying his symbolic, metaphysical polarity.

The inspector "proves" Isabelle's accusations about education; he considers it "a net of truth, which our magnificent nineteenth century has thrown over the country" (I:6). He propounds it as one of the two great tools by which humanity has conquered the human race:

> Humanity . . . has for its object, the isolation of man from this rabble of a Cosmos. . . . We give thanks to two invincible forces, the Administration and Compulsory Education. . . . The Administration isolates man's body from all places abounding in primitive virtues. It is helped in this by the municipal council and the military engineers . . . by slashing up the parks, tearing down the cloisters, erecting slate and brick offices at the feet of the cathedrals and monuments, making the sewers the true arteries of civilization, and combating the shade whenever possible, especially under trees. The man who hasn't seen the tearing down of hundred-year-old plane trees alongside the national highways hasn't seen anything! . . . and compulsory education isolates his soul. [III:1]

His views of education, quite naturally, are diametrically opposed to Isabelle's, and he has her fired. His is the authoritarian, mechanistic school.

> They [students] are not meant to be gay. If they are gay, it's because their mistress doesn't punish them enough. [I:6]
> A group of students should show their teacher the same rigid, identical face as a board of dominoes. [I:6]

Efficiency, regularity, and severity denote his educational premises. When he finds that the students write on a "blueboard" he blows up:

> Get rid of your "blueboard." And your gold chalk, pink ink, and gosling-green pencils! From now on you will have a blackboard! And black ink! And black clothes! Black, in our beautiful country, has always been the color of youth. [I:6]

The inspector is not terrifying or repulsive, even though his values are the same as those of the neo-Nazi programs of later Chaillot pimps. For Giraudoux continually deflates him by having, for example, his hat blow off when he defies the spirits, and his language break into rhyming couplets when he is demonstrating the prosaic nature of life. He is a very articulate refugee from farce. But the curious saving grace of the inspector—the reason he is more than merely bumbling—is that essentially he is right. It is a characteristic of Giraudoux's drama to put verities in the mouths of villains, and like Shaw's Undershaft, the inspector maliciously attacks romantic destiny with the one weapon that nags its way into acceptance: human truth. In this fantasy, the inspector opposes fantasy. He continually projects the values of the real world into those of the stage world, and the result is a fantasy with more solid grounding than, say, *Peter Pan*; it is a fantasy which is intellectually down to earth. If the Inspector attacks Isabelle for teaching her school-children to believe in spirits, it is because he wants them to learn the truth: "that after death there are no ghosts, . . . but only carcasses; no ghosts, only bones and maggots" (I:6). Like a rude father betraying to his child the "fact" that there is no Santa Claus, the inspector gives the children a forecast of what life has in store for them:

> I'll tell these boobies what life is like: a sad adventure with, for men,
> miserable treatment from the very beginning, tortuous advances and
> never a chance to turn back, collar buttons in revolt; and for simpletons
> like these girls, gossip and cuckoldry, saucepans and cleaning fluid. . . .
> God hasn't forseen happiness for these creatures; he has only forseen a
> few compensations—fishing, love, and senile decay. [I:6]

The inspector is as relentless as the sun, as unassailable as the inevitability of death. He is real and he is unacceptable. The druggist begs pardon from the corpse of the "ghost," "pardon because vulgarity is always right, because it is the myopic who see clearly, because there are corpses and not ghosts . . . because the inspector is right" (II:7). Giraudoux can conquer the inspector's truth only by fantastic, theatrical invention. But though ghosts may arise in the theater, such occurrences are not recorded in life, not, in any case, since the celebrated events of prior millenniums. The inspector is damnably, irresistibly right.

Fantasy is an escape from the truths of the inspector; it is one amelioration of the dialectic which man has invented for himself. As has been said of the Deity, if the world of destiny did not exist, man would have to create one. Giraudoux accepted this task unquestioningly. But fantasy cannot forge a practical, lasting bridge between the burning of destiny's sun, and the iciness of the inspector's realities. Between the worlds of humanity and destiny lies a middle ground, in which life continues. *Intermezzo* presents, as a practical compromise to the tortuous conflict, the moderate pleasures of provincial life; specifically the life of a small-town government employee. The prototype of this life is that of the *Contrôleur des Poids et Mesures* (the superintendent); he is an epitome of all that is gentle, reasonable, and, in the most rigorous sense, humanitarian. The role, which was originally played by Jouvet, was modeled frankly on the author, also a lifelong *fonctionnaire*. (The role resembles Giraudoux's father more directly; Leger Giraudoux was the *Conducteur des Ponts et Chaussées* in Bellac.)[4] The provincial setting is a pastiche of Giraudoux's childhood memories of the Limousin. He writes:

I was born in Bellac. I shall not excuse myself for having been born there. Moreover I shall not excuse myself for not having known any large town until I came of age, nor for passing my youth in five towns, none of which had more than five thousand inhabitants. The profits of this occurrence were incalculable. In sum, I was never less than a five-thousandth of each of the human agglomerations in which I resided, and twice, less than a thousandth. This makes a child certain of his size, and gives him more confidence in life.[5]

Bellac is but one of the towns where Giraudoux grew up—he speaks fondly of "le curriculum Bellac-Bessines-Pellevoisin-Cérilly-Cusset"[6]— but none is very far from the Limousin country, which is the geographical center of France, and of which Bellac is itself the geographical center. It is a beautiful yet isolated province. Giraudoux never saw a foreigner until he went to Geneva at the age of twenty, except for "two Parisians who had come for a burial and disappeared with the dead."[7] It is this provincial, very French solidarity that is nostalgically defended in *Intermezzo*. "There are three sounds which form the harmony of our province: the raking of the streets in the sleepiness of dawn, the lighting of candles after vespers, and the bugles at twilight" (I:7), says the druggist. The sounds, smells, and sights of the French countryside are continually threaded in and out of the play, which quietly, sensitively examines the particularly Gallic manner of reconciling divinities with daily life. The fullest appreciation of Giraudoux's creation must be left to those who have experienced this life. "We only beg our foreign friends to know," said one French critic, "that if the author of *Intermezzo* . . . profoundly reaches the hearts of his countrymen, it is because they recognize in the creation of his genius the magical secrets and the eternal debates, the very substance of the French soul."[8] Such simplicity is elaborated to frame and support human life.

4 Albérès, *Esthétique et morale*, p. 16.

5 "Bellac et La Tragédie," *Littérature* (Paris: Grasset, 1941), p. 285.

6 *Ibid.*, p. 286.

7 *Ibid.*, p. 286.

8 René Lalou, reviewing *La Guerre de Troie* (of which he is also speaking in the cited quotation) in *Les Nouvelles Littéraires*.

The optimism of *Intermezzo* is unmatched by any of Giraudoux's later works. Like *Siegfried* on the political level, *Intermezzo* suggests that a compromise can be found successfully between contrary demands. The young superintendent of weights and measures typifies it in his desperate appeal to Isabelle:

> Don't try to touch the limits of human life, the borders of it. Life's greatness is to be short and full between two abysses. It's miracle is to be colorful, healthy, and strong between the infinities and the voids. [II:3]

The superintendent glorifies the moderate life of the *fonctionnaire*, the excitement of trying to predict where the next assignment will come from, the daydream happiness of measuring the walk home not in meters but in leagues, as did the superintendents of the Middle Ages. He preaches the dynamics of ignorance: "An unexplained secret is nobler and more rarified than its answer.... We can rule ourselves more surely in life by virtue of our ignorances, not our revelations," he tells Isabelle (III:4). And he treats her with a kindness and consideration which, though cosmically unsatisfying, is human and husbandly. He erases the mischievous scratchings from her doorposts and he rights the overturned milk saucer by her house. Exultantly he claims to have done all a man can do; "I will have, in the smallest way, softened around Isabelle the malignity of destiny" (III:4). In a metaphysical system in which destiny is malign, the superintendent is the greatest hero of humanity. Life may be unsolvable, but it is livable. It is only necessary to keep the spirits out of man's hair, and to suppress man's greatest lust, the spiritual one.

Fitting with the earthly optimism of the predicament is a lightness of tone remarkable even for Giraudoux. The inspector cries comically to the spirits: "Asphlaroth, my most vile and ridiculous organs defy you! Not my lungs or my heart, but my gallbladder, my glottis, my sternatatory membrane!" (I:4). Details alternate between the profound and the silly. In a single sentence the superintendent speaks of "someone who would falsify our gravitation by synthesizing a new metal or discovering a new manner of sneezing" (II:3). Details are elaborated to their extremities: "when September reddens the eel pond of the Vendean marsh ... when the carriages depart from the Corner of Duguesclin and General Piquart Avenues, heading for the trotting races" (III:3). The *tirade*, a snowballing speech of tour de force literary manipulations, is used repetitively for Isabelle to describe the dead, and for the superintendent to describe the life of a *fonctionnaire*. Parody, a *tirade* with a satiric twist, is a frequent enlivening device of *Intermezzo*, particularly in the mouth of the tongue-twisted inspector.

There is a wholesale use of theatrical formats as well. In the orchestrated "Fugue for the Provincial Chorus," Giraudoux has marked "forte" and "pianissimo" in the text at appropriate places. The hangman scene is a production number which concludes with the singing of "The song of the Dandified Hangman." Both the title of the play and the final line (druggist: "*Et fini l'intermède!*") are theatrical references, and the druggist seeks to place this play in the historical tradition of the stage as he remarks, regarding Isabelle's awakening, "Now we shall see the denouement of this new episode of Faust and Marguerite" (III:6). In an earlier draft Giraudoux had even announced the theatrical framework with this extraordinary ending of the second act:

Inspector: Druggist, get us out of here. . . . You can't make me believe you
    don't have a way to pass us from ghost stories into reality!
Druggist: Yes, I have one way. But it isn't very strong.
    He makes a signal to the curtain, which falls.[9]

The literary and theatrical jangling keeps the tone of the play aloof and elegant, and prevents the audience's dwelling on the seriousness of the conflict. This was actually the direction Giraudoux was working toward, as is evidenced by the earlier version, which is considerably more realistic, more tragic, but less intriguing. *Intermezzo* is built on an intricate but shallow substructure, underlaid by a permanent disruption, and a profound probing would turn the play quickly into a morbid, self-pitying, and tedious affair.

Giraudoux intentionally keeps *Intermezzo* elusive and flighty. The unnamed Limousin town or area which is the recipient of the disturbances is called, at various times, a *bourg*, *ville*, *département*, *parage*, *région*, *arrondissement*, *canton*, *sous-préfecture*, *préfecture*, *district*, *circonscription*, *terre Limousine*, and *province*. The facts are equally vague and capricious. We might even ask, for instance, if the ghost is actually a ghost. Apparently he is only an escaped murderer for the first half of the play, for the hangmen shoot and kill him in the second act. But then why does the town become mad in the first act, and "recover" when he leaves? Giraudoux makes no attempt to answer. It is not simply a matter of carelessness or a willingness to get laughs regardless of logic, as suggested by one American critic.[10] It is an attempt to write about the illogicality of life with the illogicality of fantasy. The shifting logical premises, the inconsistencies in the plot, the intellectual sparring and backtracking are not outrages on conventional dramaturgy but an attempt to convey not only the meaning but the spirit of man adrift in the cosmic dialectic. These pesky assaults on our logical senses create, for the audience, a queasy sense of floating through fantasy as in a dream, a continuous alternation of inner and outer realities with no firm ground between them. Giraudoux provides moments of isolation rarely in his plays, and in *Intermezzo* we find more than most: the momentary peace of bugles at twilight, the street-raking at dawn. The remaining moments of logic adrift on a stormy sea contribute to the tone of mystery, fantasy, and romance which characterizes the play; they provide a subtle, funny music, which informs our senses that we can only be certain of being surprised, and will never be able to be satisfied with single, earthbound explanations. In allying subject with style, *Intermezzo* is a perfectly consistent dramatic construction.

Intermezzo may thus be considered a "perfect" play, but it is less than a great one. Theoretically and structurally it is an ideal Giraudoux creation; it is original, interesting, often exciting, and existentially truthful. The form is perfectly matched to the content. But its final impact is not profound. Although its stage history has been marked by moderate success, a few too many shared André Antoine's judgment of the 1933 opening: "mortally boring."[11] It is only infrequently revived today. The reason for this is somewhat subjective: as a romance it is simply too emotionally tepid, and as a story about human affairs it lacks human commitment. Isabelle is less than a perfect protagonist—ultimately too idealized to represent man in a near-fatal *déchirement*. The ghost, similarly, is not a strong representative of destiny. Although he is drawn with all of destiny's accoutrements—he is handsome, silent, profound, poetic, and secretive—his character is essentially anonymous and grows uninteresting. The love affair of Isabelle and the ghost is only theoretical; it is written about but it is not wholly convincing. This, finally, is the missing link of *Intermezzo*, the basic flaw of that "perfect" play.

[10] David Grossvogel, *The Self-Conscious Stage in Modern French Drama*, p. 82.
[11] "*Intermezzo* à la Comédie des Champs-Elysées," *La Petite Illustration*, no 625 (1933).

Ondine

Poke through the floating naiads and dogfish of *Ondine* and you will see the same sort of dogged depiction of man's fatal erring through a perverse universe that Sophocles portrayed in the *Oedipus Tyrannos*. "The stupidest of men always sees clearly enough to blind himself," says a character in *Ondine*, and this is the fundamental level of the play's examination. Fantasy and comic wit remove the playwright to a level of objectivity from which he boldly explores and expands the metaphysical and psychological forces that pursue man to death. It is a funny, warm, and romantic play; but it cannot be said to be compromising Giraudoux's philosophical premises one iota.

Ondine is an adaptation of the German *Märchennovelle*, *Undine*, by Friedrich de la Motte-Fouqué (1811), a story which Giraudoux had first studied at the Sorbonne. Professor Charles Andler had assigned him to prepare a commentary on *Undine* in 1909, and Giraudoux's draft for that assignment, the first preparation for *Ondine*, has been preserved.[12] The mysterious mermaid Ondines remained in Giraudoux's mind thereafter. They appear in two of his early novels,[13] and are mentioned as earlier victims of the inspector's investigations in *Intermezzo* (I:1). René Marill has found, amid the twenty-eight fragments and variations of *Intermezzo*, three pages of dialogue between Isabelle and an Ondine which Giraudoux had scribbled on the back of some diplomatic papers.[14] The Ondine world, an aquatic vision of destiny which was long nurtured in the playwright's literary thinking, came to flower in 1939 with the three-act play which we now have, a play deeply indebted to the original by La Motte-Fouqué (it is dedicated to the memory of Professor Andler), but filtered through the rare consciousness of the late-middle-aged author, now fifty-seven years old and almost a grandfather to his juvenile Ondine. Perhaps a perverse nostalgia caused Giraudoux to turn back to German mythology on the very brink of Hitler's European assaults. Dramaturgically the results

---

[12] *Die Einheit von Fouqués Undine*, published with commentary by Laurence LeSage, *Romanic Review*, 42 (1951): 122–34.

[13] *Siegfried et le Limousin* and *Aventures de Jérôme Bardini*.

[14] Albérès, *Esthétique et morale*, p. 340.

were stunning. *Ondine*, flavored by the dark passions of German romanticism, easily outperforms the gentle, logical, Gallic *Intermezzo*.

Giraudoux explains that the theme of *Ondine* is "the liaison of man with the natural elements, the flirtation of the animal world with the kingdom of man."[15] The story bears a fairly close resemblance to La Motte Fouqué's original tale. Hans, a knight errant of the Middle Ages, happens upon a cabin in the Black Forest where lives the fisherman Auguste with his wife Eugénie and their adopted daughter, Ondine. Ondine is an "undine," a beautiful young sea nymph with magical powers. Hans falls in love with her, abandons his fiancée Bertha, and brings Ondine back to the palace with him as his wife. There, however, the marriage deteriorates. Ondine, who is the ideal of beauty, purity, and love, is an unsuccessful wife, a social failure. Hans betrays her with Bertha. In revenge for the animal kingdom, the Ondine king takes Hans's life and returns Ondine to the sea. The two worlds, which were permitted to join in marriage, are once again divorced by a total separation imposed by the Ondine king. Hans cries, "Ondine and I are parting on opposite sides of eternity. On the port side nothingness, on the starboard side forgetfulness. . . . This is the first *adieu* that has been said in this base world" (III:6). As at the conclusion of *Intermezzo*, the alliance between worlds is over, and life returns to normal. But this time the protagonist has died.

The metaphysical structure of the two plays is identical but for the vital component of gender. In *Intermezzo* the protagonist is a young girl, and destiny is represented by a male spirit. In *Ondine* the protagonist is a man, and destiny is portrayed as a beautiful and spiritualized *jeune fille*. The switch in casting is extraordinary. The destiny-humanity continuum of *Ondine* is the absolute mirror of *Intermezzo's*:

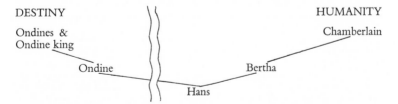

DESTINY   HUMANITY

Ondines &   Chamberlain
Ondine king

        Ondine   Bertha

                    Hans

Now it is a man who is "in the middle" and torn apart by the dialectic. "I was born to live between my stables and my dogs," cries Hans at the

[15] Yvone Moustiers' "Dans les couloirs d'un théâtre, Jean Giraudoux nous parle du roman," p. 2.

play's moving conclusion, "but no, I was caught between all nature and all destiny, like a rat" (III:6). A layer of metaphor has been removed: man in his struggle is now represented by a man, not a girl.[16] The dialectic wins. Hans, unlike Isabelle, does not survive the break. From the whimsy of *Intermezzo* Giraudoux has projected his characters into the romantic tragedy of *Ondine*.

The propulsion of *Ondine* is frankly sexual. Whereas the ghost's attractiveness for Isabelle was his superior knowledge, Ondine represents to Hans absolute sensuality. *Intermezzo* is intellectually sprung, *Ondine* appeals bodily. The Ondines cry to Hans:

> Take me, beautiful knight . . .
> Do you want me completely nude, beautiful knight? . . .
> Should I lie on my back? Should I lie on my side? . . .
>   Sometimes I think of you so strongly
>   That you squirm on your bed.
>   Still sleeping, you take my mouth,
>   And I'm brought back from the dead. [I:8]

Ondine is a nymphet well predating Lolita; for while the American translator has made her a properly sweet sixteen, Giraudoux gives her age as fourteen and a half.[17] She was born of a mass orgy of fantastic proportions. Auguste relates how he found her on the beach: "everywhere it was marked by the hollows left by two lovers embracing in the sand. But there were hundreds, thousands . . . as if a thousand couples had been copulating on the beach, and Ondine was the daughter of all of them" (I:7).[18] Ondine's nature is a direct result of such an amorous conception. Her passion for Hans knows no modesty. "Take me, transport me . . . Eat me! Complete me!" she cries to him in their first, heady meetings (I:3 and I:6). It is altogether obvious why Hans falls prey to the siren cries of the world of Ondines, and their forthright representative, Ondine: he is utterly seduced. Ondine is above all the

[16] It could be argued that this merely replaces a novel metaphor with the conventional one. But Giraudoux, as a male dramatist, is more directly involved and involving in this play than in *Intermezzo*.

[17] The translator is Maurice Valency, *Jean Giraudoux, Four Plays* (New York, 1958), p. 177. Giraudoux first describes her as fifteen (I:1) but in the second act she twice says she is "quinze ans dans un mois" (II:11). Since she has been married for three months at the time, she would have been fourteen years and eight months in the first act. The detail is unimportant as long as it is clear that Ondine is a very young girl. Actually she is not even a *jeune fille*. Giraudoux generally calls her by the same name he gives Isabelle's students in *Intermezzo: petite fille*.

[18] "Copulating" is admittedly a bit ruder than Giraudoux's "*enlacées*," but it is probably more correct in context than "embracing" or "locked together." The entire line, incidentally, is omitted in Valency's American translation.

vision of an absolute, liquid sexuality which cavorts in the minds of even the stodgiest *fonctionnaires* and foreign ministry officials.

Ondine is Giraudoux's most sublime creation of destiny; in this character he combines the vision of absolute sexuality with the beauty and terror of the *jeune fille*. The placement of Ondine on the metaphysical scale, not at the apex (as with Isabelle, Judith, and Lucile) but toward the pole of destiny, allows for this; so does the liberating form of fantasy. Ondine, though magical and fantastical, surpasses more realistic heroines in credibility. She is in harmony with the absolutes. She is beautiful; her beauty is echoed in the universe. "She is blond. Where she walks the sun follows," says Hans (II:4). She is eternal, ageless, magical, mystical. "I was born centuries ago. And I shall never die," she tells Yseult (II:11). She stays dry in the rain and can see in the blackest night. She converses lovingly with the animals and spirits, as they do with her. She creates golden ewers and mirrors out of thin air. She is loved by swineherds and kitchen maids as well as knights-errant and court poets. She is linked directly with God. "There are great forces about Ondine," says Auguste (I:7), and those forces, in *Ondine*, comprise an entire world created strictly for the play. It is a world of absolutes; absolute love, absolute beauty, absolute retribution. Compared to it, the human realm is insignificant:

> Humanity, as you call it, the place where one can forget, or change one's mind, or pardon another, occupies a very small part of the universe. In the Ondine kingdom, like the animal kingdom . . . nothing can be forgotten, and no one may be pardoned. [II:11]

Outside of her kingdom by the sea, however, Ondine's utter frankness, her "transparence" (II:11) is socially disruptive: "Our madwoman," says Eugénie (I:3); "You are mad," says Hans (I:5); "She is mad," says the chamberlain (II:9); "A madwoman! . . . What a madwoman!" says Bertha (II:10). Ondine does not read nor write. She cannot dance, she cannot ride horseback, and she cannot learn social etiquette. She cannot learn the basic rites of social behavior: how to be polite, how to lie, how to keep your mouth shut. Since the chamberlain's palm is sweaty, she is certain to make public remarks about it. Because Bertha is anxious to regain Hans, Ondine publicly accuses her. When the chamberlain tries to teach her the rituals of court behavior, she exclaims that he is teaching her how to lie. To the astonishment of the court, she tells him, "You are ugly and I hate you. There, I didn't lie that time" (II:9).

At first glance, Bertha is the exact opposite of Ondine. She is the "dark angel" (I:6) who has sent Hans into the forest to satisfy her own pride. Bertha is the perfect wife. She can memorize the thirty-four points in the first lance position, which is Giraudoux's curious way of saying she can help her husband's social standing. Ondine, when told of the thirty-four points, merely kisses Hans each time and refuses to learn. Bertha is more solid than that.

Bertha: That winter night when you told me that you still loved me, and I fled behind the mountain, you found me, followed my footprints in the snow. They were large, deep; they displayed my weariness, my despair, my love. They weren't like the scarcely visible footprints of Ondine which even the dogs couldn't see, like the wake of a ship on dry land. They were those of a woman pregnant with human life, pregnant with your future son, they were the footprints of your wife. [III:1][19]

Bertha is a woman outraged, a woman who loses her man to a vision and wants him back. Her ties to Hans are contractual, not sexual; the sexual adventure, an immediate and short-lived passion, is repellent to her. She mocks it:

Bertha: I was undoubtedly wrong in speaking of a bed. You two must sleep in the barn like peasants, on the hay. You have to brush yourself off in the morning, after your nights of love.
Hans: I can see by your words you haven't had yours yet. [II:4]

She is an unpleasant, repulsive loser. The Ondine king refers to her as having been a "little girl with a vain soul" (II:13), and when Ondine apologizes to her, she insists on being called "Highness," and forces Ondine to carry her twelve-foot train (II:12). When it is revealed that she is not a princess, but the long-lost daughter of Auguste and Eugénie, she recoils from her true parents shamefully, crying out "Don't touch me! You smell of fish!" (II:12.) Bertha may be real, but she is humanly vulgar.

The relationship between Ondine and Bertha is more complex, however, than the simple opposition of light and dark. They are connected by a permanent bond; Bertha is the sister of Ondine, as Paola is the sister of Lucile. "Bertha is my sister. My older sister," says Ondine (II:14). Bertha, too, came from the Ondine kingdom, but rejected it for the world of humanity. She still has ties to that past, a lynx at the zoo with whom she once imagined herself in love, and who still makes

[19] The light footprints were a measure of the youth and destiny-driven nature of the *jeune fille* in *Intermezzo* also.

her shiver when she sees him in his cage. But she avoids him now; "I would be wrong to see him now, on our wedding day" (III:2). Like Isabelle's superintendent, she sees no advantage in tempting destiny. She has converted; she is the older sister in the other world.

Ondine, were she human, would be in the act of conversion. Were it not for her metaphysical ties to the Ondine kingdom, she would be a *jeune femme* by the end of the play, another Bertha. "*Moi aussi, je suis bête,*" she tells Hans, as she forgives him for poaching a trout (I:5), a forgiveness which is unknown in the world of "pure" Ondines. Ondine is trying to make an alliance with the human world, to become, as she says, a "bourgeois ondine" (III:6). She tries to learn cooking and housewifery, to live by staircases, books, watches, furniture, and jewels instead of water, air, and love. She tries to give up her magical arts in return for sprains, hay fever and greasy kitchens. Symbolizing her acceptance of humanity, she insists on keeping the *collier* that Hans has given her, which the judges try to take away (III:4). The leash/collar/necklace is, of course, Giraudoux's prime symbol of the yank of humanity.[20] She is a Bertha at an earlier stage; and only the fact that she is held to destiny by force keeps her from joining her sister in a place in society. The fantasy structure, however, has kept the play clean. It has kept Ondine and Bertha eternally separate, and has isolated Hans as the protagonist in the middle of them.

Hans's course through life is the opposite of the ordinary Giraudoux etiology of idealism, disillusion, debasement, and rigidly hidden despair. Hans moves from being a stalwart, upright citizen, to a grandly spiritual, horizontal corpse. He first appears encased in armor—a physical impediment to sitting down and putting a pretty girl on his knees, an imposition of human civilization as physically repressive as the leash. He is a man "who resembles all men" (II:11). He loves to eat, to talk, to hunt. He loves war because it gives him a host of companions. In short, he is, as Ondine says, "*bête*" (I:3), with the joint connotation of bestial and stupid. "You are stupid, but you are beautiful, and all women know it. They all say, how lucky that being so beautiful he is so stupid! Because he is beautiful it will be lovely to have him in our arms, to kiss him. And it will be easy to seduce him because he is stupid" (II:10). He is the epitome of earthbound manhood.

Hans breaks from the human mold, however, when he meets Ondine in the forest. Until then he was content to lead the highly

[20] See p. 55.

regulated life of the knight-errant, accepting petty government grants for rescuing Andromedas and capturing the stolen treasures of giants. Seeing Ondine, Hans suddenly decides that his life has been a cheat, that for once he will marry the girl he finds in the forest instead of leaving her like the chivalrous Lone Ranger. "From now on I will discover, I will pillage, I will marry my captive: I will marry Ondine," he exclaims (I:7), pretty much to his own surprise. But as Ondine is a captive of her spiritual world, Hans is a captive of his earthly one, and the marriage soon becomes impossible. "His soul is too small . . . he only loves a fraction of you," Yseult tells Ondine. "You are sunlight, and he loves a blond. You are grace itself, and he loves liveliness. You are adventure, and he loves *an* adventure" (II:11). Hans quickly finds that absolute love cloys, and in panic he retreats to the safer, uglier world of Bertha and his position at the third place after the king, with the silver fork. He deceives Ondine. He imagines Ondine unfaithful to him, and divorces her. He plans to marry Bertha and has Ondine captured and put on trial. This trial, however, is the turning point of the play. Hans enters the court passionate to destroy "love." He leaves infatuated all over again. He becomes mad.

The trial is a masterpiece of Giralducien irony. To wit:

Hans: I accuse that woman of trembling in love for me, of having nothing but me for thoughts, for food, for God. Do you understand, I was her god! . . . What is your only thought, Ondine?
Ondine: You.
Hans: What is your bread? What is your wine? When you sat at our table and raised your goblet, what did you drink?
Ondine: You.
Hans: What is your god?
Ondine: You.
Hans: You hear that, you judges! She pushes love to the point of blasphemy! [III:4]

Hans begs for surcease from the spiritual world; release from the tensions of absolutism. He has been victimized by his own lusts, and he seeks to still them. The trial becomes a philosophical debate:

Judge: We are judging an Ondine, not love.
Hans: But that's what this trial is all about. Thats what's before the bar; love with its ribboned tail. . . . I accuse the truest love of being the falsest, the most ecstatic love of being the vilest . . . [III:4]

"We are swimming in incoherence, Knight," responds one of the judges. Hans's accusations fall apart. It was not Ondine who was unfaithful or deceptive, it was himself. Ondine was faithful. It is human love which is perverse and superficial. Hans is abashed, humiliated. He can no longer bear Bertha, or himself. He is too altered by destiny to again accept the hypocrisy of human love—even of his own love. He begins to falter as the human encasement crumbles. He begins to hear poetry in the words of his servants. The sixty-year-old kitchen girl appears; he says that she is beautiful. "He is mad," remarks a judge (III:4). Hans begins a rapid descent into the world of destiny. To him, his horse speaks:

Maître, chéri, adieu
je te rejoins en dieu. [III:5]

Not only has he regained a spiritual alliance with animals, now they speak to him in verse. With heavy irony, the king of Ondines describes him to Ondine: "He wanders in the castle. He talks to himself. He rambles. That's the way of men who have withdrawn from themselves, when they have slammed against a truth, a simplicity, a treasure. They become what is called mad. They are suddenly logical, they no longer deny themselves, they don't marry women they don't love. They have the reasoning of the plants, of the waters, of God: they are mad . . . he is mad. He loves you!" (III:5.)

Hans's descent into destiny and death is pathetic but admirable. Isabelle rose from her coma into the life-giving arms of her superintendent, but we feel she has been betrayed. Hans falls from Bertha's clutches and we feel that he has won. This is no reaction against heterosexuality; it is a response to the structures of contractual society, in this case marriage and compromise. The final scene, the ultimate parting of Hans and Ondine, is one of Giraudoux's most beautiful moments, and its effect on contemporary audiences was enormous, and has even become legendary. Hans greets Ondine with a continuation of their first love scene in Act One; thus:

Ondine: Moi, on m'appelle Ondine.
Hans: C'est un joli nom. [I:5]

Hans: Moi, on m'appelle Hans!
Ondine: C'est un joli nom. [III:6]

A lifetime has been added with that exclamation point. Hans pities himself ironically, wondering why, of all men, he was the one selected to be torn apart by the shattering forces of destiny.

Hans: Why do you always make the same mistake, you who are called Artemis, or Cleopatra, or Ondine! The men who are made for love are little professors with big noses, fatlipped landlords, bespectacled Jews: those who have the time for it, who enjoy it, who can suffer for it. No! You soar down on a poor general like Antony, on a poor knight like Hans, on any miserable, middling human being. Then it's all over for him. As for me, I haven't had a moment to myself, with the wars, looking after my animals, hunting and trapping! No, you had to come and add fire to my veins, poison to my eyes, a whiff of bile in my mouth. From heaven to hell I was shaken, battered, flayed alive. . . . It wasn't very fair. [III:6]

The drama, metaphysical in form, is psychological in import. There is truth in the original remark of Auguste, that "Ondine is a dream! There is no Ondine" (I:7). Ondine exists because Hans dreams of her. Ondine is the fire in his blood and the carnal taste in his mouth. She is his nagging dissatisfaction with Bertha and his awareness of the folly of human mendacity. The cry of Hans is of a man distraught at himself, a man internally split between the desirability of what he cannot have and the pettiness of what he does have.

The metaphysical expansion has not altered the Giraudoux philosophy, which has been consistent from *Siegfried* to *Electra* to *Sodom and Gomorrah*. What it has done is to give it a bold, theatrical expression. The crux of *Electra's* dichotomy between human justice and absolute justice[21] is made in *Ondine* more theatrical than intellectual:

Judge: Bertram disappeared six months ago. Human justice is unable to bring him back.
Ondine King: That's because it isn't really very strong.
    Voila! (Bertram suddenly appears.) [III:4]

Absolute justice appears in the world of fantasy as big as life. What better medium than the theater to express it? Destiny is created structurally in *Ondine*, it is not merely described or implied. The romance of a pure, intercosmic love affair tested Giraudoux's talents in a traditional but effective medium. The ironic wit is never absent, but the rhythms of the dialogue, the orchestrally repeated phrases and images, the depth of characterization, and above all, the sensuality of the passion, has made

[21] See chap. 3.

the Hans-Ondine love affair an actable, credible, poetic romance.[22]
It is the only play of Giraudoux's that is popularly considered a love
story, and this popular conception is the proper one. The poetry and
the corporeality of the love affair complement each other. If psychological reality makes the metaphysics move, poetry keeps the romance
from becoming sentimental. "How I would have loved him!" says
Ondine with sad, cruel, dramatic irony as she looks at the corpse of the
forgotten Hans at the final moment of the play (III:7). Underneath,
Giraudoux is still perversely gay; he still plays his jokes on mankind.
Like Jean and Lia, death is not enough—destiny still keeps talking.

The romantic propulsion of Ondine is always kept in check by the
witty satire on human society; a satire which is properly revealing
what it is attacking.

Chamberlain: The court is a holy place where man must keep complete
   control over the two traitors which can betray him: his word and his
   face. If he is afraid, he should show courage. If he lies, frankness. It
   isn't even a bad idea, if you have to speak the truth, to assume the air
   of speaking false. This gives the truth that equivocal aspect which
   disadvantages it the least against hypocrisy. [II:9]

The chamberlain, another right-wing extremist in the line of *Intermezzo's* inspector, gently prods Ondine with the truths of human
behavior. Lying is also known, he reminds her, by the more acceptable
name of politeness.

Chamberlain: Understand, please, that politeness is a way of reserving your
   place, the best way! When you get older, thanks to politeness, people
   will say that you are young. When you are ugly, they will say that
   you are beautiful, all this with a minimum investment.
Ondine: I will never get older . . . [II:9]

Perhaps unnecessary for mermaids, politeness, the telling of lies, is part
of the accepted fabric of social life. Expressed in this way, Giraudoux
has extended comic fun from a relatively unexamined bit of common

---

[22] This is less evident in Maurice Valency's translation, which until recently was the
only available English version, and which was performed on Broadway and elsewhere in
America between 1939 and 1967. Valency emasculates Hans considerably, and tones down
the fervidness of Ondine and the entire romance. He eliminates the important details of
the sexuality of the conflict, such as the orgiastic events surrounding Ondine's birth. To
his credit, Valency admits to being an adapter, rather than a translator; still it is difficult to
understand why one must so compulsively rewrite the work of an established playwright
such as Giraudoux. If cutting is necessary for performance, at best that is a job for the
individual director.

behavior. The comic satire is generally expressed in this sort of paradox, for example:

Ondine: I am his mistress, yes his mistress! Don't you understand that?
That's the name men have for their wives. [I: 5]

Ondine: You are very modest, in your vanity . . . [II: 9]

Fisherman: Her voice is marvelous, her skin is like silk, she is ravishing:
she must be the monster!" [III: 2]

Paradox is simply the juxtaposition of one world with the other in the
same sentence; in *Ondine* it is almost the sole comic medium of the
author. It is an upside down kingdom in which the slightest draft of
fantasy can reverse the course of human events—can make the blind
man see, and then seeing, die. It describes the plunge from sanity to
insanity as the climb to the pinnacle of godly wisdom as opposed to
man's. It acts comically and tragically in the same breath, mixing the
genres in a poetic, cruel, and absurd vision of human fatality. The combination is a rare piece of theater.

   Ondine is a play that carries its own dramaturgical analysis in its
middle. Much of the second act is a polemical discussion of theater,
which includes no less than five plays-within-a-play, including two
that occur simultaneously; a cacophony of *Salammbô*, and the ritualized
revelation of Bertha's "expulsion." The first three plays are a compression of the sequence of events by which Hans returns to Bertha.
The compression is the magical art of the Ondine king in disguise as
an "illusionist without material" (II: 1), and it is greatly appreciated
by the Court and the chamberlain, who remarks that "life is a play
which simply lingers on. It needs a stage manager to an incredible
degree. . . . The great advantage of the theater over life is that it
doesn't smell rancid" (II: 1). This is essentially Giraudoux's position
regarding *Ondine*. The sensitive poet criticizes the hastening of events.
"It's a terrible thing to accelerate life! You suppress its two saving
elements: distractions and idleness" (II: 1). The argument holds for
life perhaps, but not for the theater. *Ondine's* structural power is its
cleanliness, its speed, its breadth. Giraudoux does not permit himself
to linger over the internal split within man—he ignites his imagination
with the problem and lets it fly into sparkling worlds. By contrast,
Intermezzo is lazy. *Ondine* is awash with nude Venuses, disappearing and
appearing phantoms, out-of-nowhere production numbers (such as
the trial scene), and the frank use of songs, poetry, and choruses throughout the three acts. The five plays-within-the-play jar the spectator into

various states of confusion and awareness. The settings are a designer's dream. No play of Giraudoux's is more theatrically composed than *Ondine*, and none exhibits such a range of dramaturgic conceits and devices.

The theatricality of *Ondine* keeps the dilemma from "smelling rancid," but not at the expense of honesty. In fact, the theatricality emphasizes the more serious themes. It represents, in its combination of fantasy, magic, and poetry, the ineffable world of destiny, the bewildering universe. The play-within-a-play is another exercise in oscillating perspectives of reality, and focuses the audience's attention on the human reality of the protagonist, Hans. The traditional use of the play-within-a-play is to enhance the credibility of the actor in the "first" play; that is, Hamlet in *Hamlet* is never more credible than when he is watching the "players" perform in *The Murder of Gonzago;* it is as though Hamlet stepped out into the audience with us to watch it. When he compares himself and his emotions to the players, we believe he is one of us. Giraudoux compounds the perspectives with the use of simultaneous plays-within-a-play at varying levels of credibility: Hans, the observer of each, gains our sympathy and trust. The theatricality of the Ondine kingdom and the court emphasizes by contrast the reality of Hans and his human predicament.

Hans observes himself and his situation from the theatrical perspective. "That's the title, *Ondine*. It's going to be called *Ondine*, this story in which I appear here and there like an imbecile, stupid as a man" (III:6). He is openly metaphoric, for he is speaking not of himself alone, but of his race. He, like the audience in the theater, is attempting to understand a chaotic universe. He is experiencing unexplained phenomena. When he dies, the audience knows they share this fate. The theatricalism of *Ondine* does not remove the audience from human dilemmas, but it expounds and expands them in a fairy-tale mirage. The tragedy is delicately sensed throughout and lends the palatable work a terrible reality.

At the play's end, one is left lingeringly aware of that reality. Jean Anouilh, whose own work is deeply indebted to Giraudoux's, has written of the original production:

When Jouvet [Hans] lay down in his black armor upon that long grey stone, a despair rent me which I shall never forget. It was not only too beautiful, it not only made ridiculous everything I had wanted to do, it was tender, solemn, and definitive, like a farewell. I had a very certain feeling about it: the farewell of Hans to Ondine took on the meaning of another farewell which wrenched my heart. It was the time of the phony war and we dreamt about lives in danger. I believed, naively, that this mysterious farewell concerned me.[23]

Another author, Marcel Moussy, has described that last farewell as a "majestic anguish."[24] It was as strong an effect as Giraudoux had ever created, even in plays much more "serious" in tone. It cannot be said that *Ondine* is a tragedy, since that word describes a dramatic form for which tradition dictates numerous specifications that *Ondine* fails to follow. But it is undeniably tragic. "The tragic excludes neither gaiety nor laughter,"[25] Giraudoux claimed, and neither the romance, nor the fantasy, nor the theatricality of *Ondine* can disfigure the tragic structure of the theme. *Ondine* is built upon the same premises as *Phèdre*: that love is poison in man's blood, and the fate which brings it is malign. Hans is thematically prefigured by the Racinian tragic heroine Phèdre, who cries:

> Ce n'est plus une ardeur dans mes veines cachées,
> C'est Vénus tout entière à sa proie attachée.[26]

Like Phèdre, Hans was the prey of gods who summoned from his blood the passions which led him lusting to his death.

The Apollo of Bellac

The Apollo of Bellac is metaphysical only in a very limited sense. The almost-love affair between Agnès, a *jeune fille*, and Apollo, the Greek god of beauty, is only a small part of this short work, which is otherwise a frothy jest, set in a modern Parisian business office. The mystery and fantasy of *Ondine* and *Intermezzo* are almost completely missing. Nonetheless it is the Agnès-Apollo love affair which is at the heart of the play's structure, and *The Apollo of Bellac* continues—actually concludes—Giraudoux's series of dramatic speculations involving the romancing of man by the spirits of destiny.

---

[23] "To Jean Giraudoux," p. 3.
[24] "Jouvet ou Giraudoux?" *Cahiers de la Compagnie.*
[25] André Warnod, "J'ai épousseté le buste d'Electre, nous dit M. Jean Giraudoux."
[26] *Phèdre*, I: 3.

Originally known as *The Apollo of Marsac*, the one-act play was the last work of Giraudoux's to be first seen in Paris under the authority of Louis Jouvet. Jouvet, who had added it to his company's repertoire in Rio de Janeiro in 1942, premiered it in Paris in 1947 with Jean Genêt's *The Maids* as the curtain riser. It was admittedly an exotic combination. *The Maids* is a miasma of sexual perversity, Artaudian cruelty, and ritualized murder; *The Apollo of Marsac* was Giraudoux's return to the gentleness and ironic gaiety of *Intermezzo* and *Amphitryon 38*. Still, it was an opportunity for the past to take hands with the present, a meeting not without sympathetic vibrations in each, as is discussed in the final chapter. But in 1947, *The Apollo* was profoundly of the past.

The play is a digression on the first line uttered by Ondine in the earlier play. As Ondine enters the cabin and sees Hans for the first time, she boldly exclaims: "How beautiful you are!" (*Ondine*, I:3). The audacity and simplicity of that remark pierce Hans's armor with a terrible shock. Auguste and Eugénie are properly scandalized. They tell Ondine that she is boring her guest; she rightly replies that she is not boring him, she is pleasing him. Nothing could be more truthful; Hans is utterly bowled over. Although Ondine goes on to call him stupid, (*une bête*) he is not dissuaded from loving her; the naïve fourteen-year-old who said directly what others had, for reasons of social etiquette, forbidden themselves to speak aloud has made herself irreversibly a part of his life. Hans is delighted in his confusion:

> She made me unhappy because I *am* "une bête" as she calls it.
> At heart we men are all the same, as vain as guinea hens.
> When she said I was beautiful—well, I know I'm not beautiful
> but she made me happy. [I:4]

The magical phrase can unlock the stubbornest hearts. *Ondine*, of course, goes on to examine the ensuing love affair; *The Apollo of Bellac* lingers over the moment of unlocking.

Agnès is the youthful heroine-protagonist of *The Apollo*, and she is described in a stage direction of an early version as being a young woman "with a singular resemblance to Madeleine Ozeray,"[27] who had originally created the role of Ondine. Agnès in *The Apollo* bears less resemblance to Ondine, however, than she does to the Agnès of Molière's *L'École des Femmes*. Mlle Ozeray had not only played Agnès

[27] *Théâtre Complet*, 14 (variantes III): 101.

in Jouvet's celebrated production of that play,[28] but Giraudoux, in his rehearsal play *Paris Impromptu*, had allowed her to play herself playing Molière's Agnès. Like Molière's heroine, Giraudoux's Agnès is a shy, pretty, *jeune fille*, who likes men but seems unable to get the hang of them. When they look at her, or talk to her, she feels faint. As the play opens, she is being unceremoniously brushed aside by a clerk at the "Office of Big and Small Inventions," where she has come to look for a job but has been afraid even to explain her wants. To her immediate aid comes a mysterious "man from Bellac," who takes her aside and explains to her the one secret of success with men: simply tell them that they are beautiful. She does, and right away all doors begin to open. The clerk invites her to see the president, and puts in a good word for her. The secretary general offers her a job, and ignores her admission that she cannot type or take dictation. The president fires his secretary, dismisses his fiancée, and proposes to marry her. "It works?" asks Agnès. "Too well," replies the man from Bellac, "I have unchained the devil" (I:7).

This intriguing comic idea gives rise to one of Giraudoux's cleverest comedies, underlaid with a cogent set of observations on the vanity of men. "Each man, even the ugliest, keeps alive in himself one secret place, which directly reunites him with absolute beauty," the man from Bellac tells Agnès (I:5), and the woman who will gain man's undying affection is the woman who will "pronounce, simply and loudly, that word that he is continually whispering to himself" (I:5). It is doubtless an accurate observation, which the course of dramatic events comically affirms. The man teaches Agnès to speak the words Ondine first spoke to Hans: "How beautiful you are." And he teaches her to speak them boldly and unequivocably. She practices on a butterfly, on a bust of Archimedes, on a chandelier (which lights) and on the man from Bellac himself, who coaches her. "You're hinting! You're hinting! ... You're still hinting!" he keeps telling her when she is too oblique. (I:4, I:5.) His goal is frankness, and when Agnès learns it, she becomes worldlywise and confident.

There are actually two stories in *The Apollo of Bellac* which result from this predication. The first is the president's selecting Agnès over both his icy secretary Chèvredent (Goat-tooth) and his mistress-fiancée, Thérèse. As he tells the crabby secretary, "I have the choice between spending my days with a frightful person who finds me ugly

[28] Jouvet's production of *L'Ecole des Femmes* opened in 1936 and eventually played 446 performances.

and a ravishing one who finds me beautiful. Draw your own conclusions." Chèvredent does. "You're going to replace me with that mad girl?" she cries. "Right away" says the president (I:7). The president's choice of wives is a similar but more elaborate one: between the naïve Agnès, who has velvet chairs in her home and who tells him he is handsome, and the "humanity" figure, Thérèse, who has scratchy Directoire chairs in her home and tells him he is ugly. Again the president selects Agnès, the pretty child who tells him what he wants to hear, Thérèse's claims of more efficient home management notwithstanding. The dialectic is pretty obvious:

Thérèse: And may I require why Agnès is replacing Chèvredent?
President: Because Agnès finds me beautiful.
Thérèse: Are you going mad?
President: No, becoming beautiful.
Thérèse: Do you know what you were this morning?
President: This morning I was a man with bowed legs, a sickly complexion, and decaying teeth. I was what you saw me as.
Thérèse: I still see you.
President: Yes, but Agnès sees me too. I prefer her eyesight. [I:8]

Thérèse claims Agnès is lying. The Man from Bellac, another "mad" man according to her, comes forward to explain. "The truth is that all men are beautiful, and always beautiful, and the woman who tells them that is not lying." "You're ugly!" Thérèse insists to the president. "You're ugly. My entire being cries it out to you . . . it cries to tell you the truth . . . Why are you all against me!" The man from Bellac tells her: "It's your own fault! Your crime! How do you expect the president to be beautiful when you, when his entire surroundings, keep repeating to him that he is ugly!" (I:8.) It is a worthy argument. Beauty is in the eye of the beholder, and what man has not the right, when he has the chance, to choose his own beholder?

The president's choice is similar to that of Hans, if we put aside the fantasy: whether to accept the pure, young, naïve *jeune fille*, who likes comfortable chairs and fresh flowers, or the elegant, proper, coldly efficient *femme noire* who represents the *jeune fille* at a later stage. The irony of the situation is simply that Agnès must someday lose her naïveté, and the president will be right back where he started. As soon as she wins the president from Thérèse, the man from Bellac notes that she looks "a little fatter" than she did moments ago (I:9), and there is no doubt where this course will lead. Nonetheless it is equally true that reality is too difficult to define by any one mirror: that being the case, the president may as well accept Agnès's version as Thérèse's. Neither woman is telling "the truth," both are reflecting what they see through the filter of what they want to see. This is simply the confused nature of human perception. The president has the right to pick the mirror that flatters him the most, but he had best be aware that human mirrors are more changeable than glass ones.

The second story is a bit more complex, and takes the simple fable into the realm of fantasy. The president having selected Agnès, it is now up to her to select him. The rivalry here is not a mere earthly opponent but a divine one: Agnès must select between the president and the man from Bellac, who seems to be Apollo, the Greek god of supreme beauty in an earthly disguise. Like Jupiter in *Amphitryon 38*, Apollo has come down to the world of man to offer divine happiness to a young woman —an affair with destiny. Agnès must close her eyes to see him, his beauty is so overpowering. "I have poor eyes," she tells Apollo, "They weren't made to see the supreme beauty. It would destroy them." Apollo offers himself to Agnès but she refuses him. She is a willing captive to the world of humanity and the pettiness that such a life entails. She rejects beauty, with its "implacable" eyesight, in favor of her completely ordinary daily life:

> Don't count too much on me, supreme beauty. You know, I have a very little life. My day is completely mediocre. Each time I go back to my room I have to climb five flights of steps, through the shadows and the smells of burning fat. Whether I'm going to work or to sleep, that same preface of five flights awaits me. I'm all by myself! Sometimes, happily, a cat waits by the doorway. I pet it. A milk bottle has overturned. I right it. If I smell gas I alert the concierge. . . . That's my life! It is flesh and shadow pressed together, a little bit bruised. [I:9]

This is the defense of the humdrum human condition outlined by the superintendent of *Intermezzo*, who also found his pleasures in life by petting a cat on its window on his way home and righting Isabelle's milk pail outside her door (*Intermezzo* III:4). It is an acceptance of the strictures of being human, with the compromises that they entail. When Electra smelled leaking gas, she went after it "until the world cracked and crumbled to its very foundations, and its generations of generations, and until thousands of innocents died an innocent death . . ." (*Electra* I:13). When Agnès smells gas, she alerts the concierge. It is an adult way to live, a gentle compromise.

Agnès, unlike Isabelle, does not need to be convinced of the necessity of accepting humanity; she is already sold. She refuses the god of beauty, with his golden ringlets and gilded halo, because he is too pure for her, too dazzling for her world.

Agnès: You are too brilliant, too grand for my stairway. The one whom I cannot hold to me in my stairway is not the one for me. . . . Go away, Apollo!

Apollo: If I disappear you will find a human, mediocre like yourself . . .

Agnès: That's my lot. I prefer it. . . . Disappear.

Apollo disappears. "Is Apollo here?" asks one of the businessmen. "No, he has passed," says Agnès in the concluding lines of the play (I:9).

There is an undeniable trace of sadness in the play's conclusion, a sadness which once again echoes Holofernes' prediction that "young girls are made for monsters . . . but they are given to men. From then on their lives are wrecked" (*Judith* II:7). Agnès is left to marry the president, a man who she admits is ugly (to Apollo, I:9), and who is certainly a stolid citizen in the world of humanity. He is even more "civilized" than Isabelle's superintendent, for he is Parisian and bureaucratic. The provincial life is to the left (destiny) side of Paris; it is represented in *The Apollo* by a human form, a man from Bellac. The sadness in the play[29] guarantees its trueness to the basic principles of Giraudoux's thought, that life is a fatal course toward compromise and debasement. But the comic treatment illustrates Giraudoux's greatest gift, to be able to make light of the dire consequence of being born. The evocation of beauty, of provincial warmth, of a romantic spirit, and the demasking of male vanity provides an unusually rich combination in the one-act form. *The Apollo of Bellac* is one of Giraudoux's most charming works, and demonstrates once more the variety of dramatic experience which can be nurtured from an unvarying philosophical look at the world and the cosmos about it.

[29] A sadness, incidentally, which Valency has eliminated from the English version by creating a new character, "the Chairman of the Board," who is *really* handsome (in the eyes of the audience and Agnès), one to whom Agnès never needs to say the magic line in order to captivate. Valency also eliminates Apollo's remark about Agnès's getting "a little fatter" after her conquest, and makes Thérèse return to the president after learning a lesson. Agnès then may wholesomely marry the chairman.

Siegfried—1928

The Trojan War Will Not Take Place—1935

Electra—1937

The Madwoman of Chaillot—1943
(premiered in 1945)

Three

THE POLITICAL PLAYS

The metaphysical plays are an expansion, theatrically, of the ideas in the sexual plays; destiny, which is man's lust for purity and absolute sensuality, is elaborated into a world of ghosts, fishes, gods, and supergods. The political plays represent a different sort of expansion of the same intellectual scheme: an expansion not into the cosmos but into society. The political plays examine the same divorce between man's destiny and his human situation, but the specific battlefields are political: France versus Germany, war versus peace, human justice versus *justice intégrale*, and mechanism versus individualism. These are the substance of another tetralogy of plays, the political tetralogy, which includes *Siegfried*, *The Trojan War Will Not Take Place*,[1] *Electra*, and *The Madwoman of Chaillot*. These four plays are very tightly interconnected. They span Giraudoux's entire playwrighting career—*Siegfried* was his first play and *Madwoman* about his last—and are closely tied with his social and political concerns throughout this period.

It is easy to forget that Giraudoux was a lifelong official in the French government and a dedicated servant of his country. Certainly he never wore the badge of the *engagé* with as much ostentation as did several of his contemporaries. Yet this aspect of his work has been much ignored. Yves Lévy wrote, in an article entitled "Giraudoux and Social Problems,"

The posthumous destiny of Giraudoux is a strange one, strange because the writer has been interpreted not according to his nature, but according to the idea that others have made of him. . . . One critic, some years ago, analyzing some of Giraudoux's expressions, noticed in his work—rightly or wrongly—

[1] Known in the English-speaking world in Christopher Fry's translation, *Tiger at the Gates*.

an Aristotelian penchant. Since then it is impossible to speak of him without the qualification "precious."[2]

The critic in question, of course, is Sartre. Preciosity had been noticed in the writings of Giraudoux long before Sartre got around to it,[3] but in the tumultuous years surrounding the Second World War preciosity had become the opposite of engagement, and seemed to border on the cowardly. To be Aristotelian when the Luftwaffe was bombing Rotterdam, Sartre seemed to be saying, was indefensible ivory-towerism, and this is a charge which Giraudoux left unrefuted at his death in 1944.

The facts of Giraudoux's personal commitment to his country's cultural and political future are no longer in doubt. As the servant of France in the Ministry of Foreign Affairs, as the political essayist whose pieces appeared almost annually from *Retour d'Alsace* in 1917 to *Sans Pouvoirs* in 1945, Giraudoux was one of France's most vital public philosophers. In his well-read essays, according to Lévy, "the social problems of our times and of our country are examined with a controlled passion which vibrates with the profoundest public concerns.[4] In his public utterances and radio broadcasts, said another of his countrymen, "Giraudoux is one of us, he is the herald of the best in each of us. . . . Giraudoux is one of the most perfect filters which now dispenses the French conscience."[5] What has been and still is questioned however, is Giraudoux's political commitment in the literary work, and how the man who wrote the eloquent "Future of France,"[6] could, at the same time, engage in the whimsical fantasies of *The Madwoman of Chaillot*. To the nature of Giraudoux's literary commitment this chapter is largely devoted, and while there is no intention to dispose of such masterpieces as *Electra* and *The Trojan War* as simply *pièces à clef*, it is clear that to disassociate these works from the political influences which affected them is to get so involved with the champagne as to forego the Châteaubriand.

[2] "Giraudoux et les problèmes sociaux," p. 7.

[3] The first important review of Giraudoux's work, André Gide's note on his *Provinciales*, remarked on its "preciosities," which, Gide noted, were "happily . . . infrequent." *La Nouvelle Revue Française*, June 1, 1909, p. 465.

[4] Lévy, "Giraudoux et les problèmes sociaux," p. 8.

[5] A. M. Petitjean, "Quand Jean Giraudoux parle du deuil et de l'espoir de la France."

[6] "L'Avenir de France," in *Sans Pouvoirs* (Monaco: Le Rocher, 1946), pp. 125–50.

Siegfried

Siegfried is the first of Giraudoux's political plays, also his first play, and of all his plays it is the most contemporary and the most "realistic." These facts, considered together, are significant. Giraudoux's entry into dramatic literature was with a personal, actually autobiographical statement of his most common political theme, the uneasy relationship between France and Germany in the modern world. Gradually, in his succeeding plays, he managed to recover this subject in newer theatrical upholstery. But seen relatively bare on its first appearance, *Siegfried* is a refreshingly direct play.

It was originally written as a novel, entitled *Siegfried et le Limousin*, and when it appeared in 1922, its author was already well known within the Parisian literary circle. He had not, at that time, any experience in or with the theater,[7] but after making a trial adaptation of his *Siegfried* for the stage, he was encouraged to seek possibilities for making it into a film. To this end he got in touch with Bernard Zimmer, a Boulevard playwright, who introduced him to Jouvet. The meeting with Jouvet apparently convinced Giraudoux to attempt a full-scale stage dramatization, which he presented to Jouvet in 1928, and which Jouvet produced at his Théâtre des Champs-Elysées that spring. Not only Giraudoux's future career as a dramatist, but the entire contemporary French theater can be said to date from this production, beginning also the famous collaboration between the author and the *homme du théâtre*.

Like the novel, the story of *Siegfried* (the remainder of the original title, along with a dozen-odd characters and episodes from the novel, was omitted in the play) concerns Jacques Forestier, a French poet, who is wounded in the First World War. Left naked and unconscious on the battlefield, he awakes in a state of total amnesia, completely bereft of all vestiges of identity. He is nursed back to health by Eva, the svelte German Fräulein who teaches him to speak again—but it is

---

[7] In *Visitations* (Paris 1947) Giraudoux describes his only theatrical experiences prior to *Siegfried*: acting in original miracle plays with his cousins from the country when he was a young boy.

German that he learns. In the past seven years he has become Siegfried von Kleist, first citizen of Gotha, chancellor of Germany, the proponent of a model constitution, and the leader of rational liberalism and democracy. Still, he searches to find his former identity, and his former friends seek to find him—particularly his French mistress, the sculptress Geneviève, who comes to Gotha to reclaim him for herself and for France. This is the point at which the play begins, and obviously Giraudoux has created a story of great dramatic excitement. But, as he explains, "my drama begins where the melodrama ends" (I:6), and the plot soon gives way to a skeletal network of ideas on which the entire Franco-German cultural and political struggle is displayed.

The structure of the political plays is more complex than the metaphysical ones, and while it follows the same form—an inverted, three-tiered pyramid—there are additional internal antitheses. For *Siegfried*, Giraudoux placed his characters in this multilevel relationship, with the conflicting notions of France and Germany at the top levels, and man, the unwilling apex, at the bottom:

DESTINY   HUMANITY

French destiny   French rationality   German destiny   German rationality
(Forestier)   (Robineau)   (Zelten)   (Siegfried)

         FRANCE   GERMANY

        (Geneviève)   (Eva)

                       MAN

           (Forestier-Siegfried)

Each tier of the pyramid is an antithesis, an opposition between equal but opposite antagonists. The middle tier, the heartland of the play and the one which received the most contemporary attention, is the antithesis between "France" and "Germany." These we must put in quotation marks, since Giraudoux speaks not only of the countries but of the idea of Frenchness and Germanness. On this level of ideological conflict we find Siegfried, "upon whom destiny is prepared to strike" (III:2), the protagonist forced to choose between opposite countries, each represented by a characteristic mistress. The contrast between them is the contrast between France and Germany. "Eva is an exclamation point, she gives bright, emphatic sense to everything around her. You, Geneviève, with your calm, your simplicity, are a question mark," says Siegfried (II:5). Germany is a country of towering magnitude and wild boorish eclecticism, where the movie house is a

Greek temple, the museum is a medieval castle, and the palace is named for Maximilian and designed as a Florentine palazzo. France, we are shown, is a country of rural villages, small churches, and quiet, mysterious people. "Choose, Siegfried," says Eva. "Choose, Jacques," says Geneviève (III:5).

The choice, however, is illusory. Forestier finally elects to return to France, irrespective of any moral preference for that country. It is impossible to make a moral choice between "France" and "Germany" because each is merely an abstraction; outwardly definable only by a style of architecture, a manner of speaking, a few types of vegetation, a few variations of climate. The inward and essential nature of each country is in a continuous process of redefinition. Giraudoux quickly goes beyond the France-Germany conflict to a complex, fourfold antithesis: German destiny versus German pragmatism on the one hand and French charm versus French bureaucracy on the other. It is only by the conflict of internal forces that the abstractions of "France" and "Germany" can be accurately portrayed, and Giraudoux, in broadening his perspective, goes well beyond clichéd interpretations.

He regards Germany as locked in an internal struggle between the old and the new, between the dark medieval romanticism which inspired Goethe, Dürer and Beethoven, and the contemporary mechanized Prussianism, which, distorted, inspired Kaiser Wilhelm and Adolf Hitler. For his representative of Old Germany, Giraudoux has created the character of Zelten, actually "Otto-Wilhelmus von Zelten-Buchenbach." New Germany is represented by Siegfried and his allied, intense generals, Fontgeloy, Waldorf and Ledinger. The struggle is ideological and tinged with the fantastic. Zelten, a wild, Bavarian romantic, occupies his spare time reenacting famous German suicides, and losing himself in his effort to prevent Germany from becoming a "*société anonyme*." He claims that "Germany is not a social and human enterprise: it is a poetic conjuration of spirits!" (I:2) and he rejects the forces of "Morgan Rockefeller," which can throw Germany into a panic by threatening to cancel the "artificial phosphate contract." However, Zelten's revolutionary army, supported only by the "cubists and cocaine addicts," is overthrown by Siegfried and the generals, and Zelten is forced into exile, lamenting the centralization and bureaucracy which Siegfried will initiate. "I persist in thinking that the true Germans still love their little kingdoms and their over-sized passions," Zelten says, admitting that "you have taken me *in flagrante delicto* with Germany. Yes, I have slept with her, Siegfried.

I am still full of her perfume, that odor of dust and rose petals and blood which she gives off whenever someone touches one of her sovereignties; I have had everything she gives to her lovers, the drama, the power over souls. She will never give you anything but an agricultural compound" (III:2).

Zelten's outlook is soaring, sensual, and wildly illogical in the ordinary sense; it is the reinforced echo of Richard Wagner. Modern Germany, planned by the rational Siegfried, is organized and coldly official. As Zelten explains it,

> A model of social order, with the thirty little kingdoms, the duchies, the free towns suppressed, and with them their thirty different vibrations of culture and liberty; in their places I see a country broken into equilateral jurisdictions [*Départements*] whose only adventures will be budgetary planning, life insurance, and old age annuities; in short, a nation as theoretical as Siegfried, without a memory and without a past. [I:2]

The past of Germany was Bavarian, the future will be Prussian; and Zelten, for Giraudoux, decries the process. Germany cannot be so rigidly organized, maintains Zelten, for "every time a German has tried to make Germany into a practical edifice, his work has ultimately crumbled into scattered reflections" (I:2). For Germany to live without its magnificent heritage would not only be reprehensible, it would be impossible, claims Zelten, and our present perspective nearly forty years after this statement does little to alter its wisdom.

The problem of Germany's future was not merely an academic one with Giraudoux, for he was deeply involved in it on the personal level. *Siegfried*, in fact, is in many ways directly autobiographic. In the novel, Giraudoux assumes the voice of the first person, the character "Jean," who, like Giraudoux himself, was one of a few French scholarship students sent to Germany for a year's study. In the play, the character of Jean is missing, but Giraudoux represents himself in the personnage of Robineau, a gentle French philologist who shares Giraudoux's actual first name (Hippolyte), and like him, is described as having first come to Germany before the war "in a raid of twelve Sorbonne students whom France released victoriously . . . on the Saxon dialects" (I:5). Giraudoux's experience in Germany had been overwhelming, and when he had returned to Paris in those prewar days, it was to complete a doctoral degree in German literary studies. Following this, Giraudoux was wounded in service at the Alsatian front, an experience which he blamed on Prussianism, while writing nostalgically of the beauty of Alsace. He refused to hold "Germany" culpable. Politically committed to a rapprochement with Germany after the war—a controversial position in interwar French diplomacy—Giraudoux felt above all the danger of Prussianism, under the guise of modernity, taking hold of Germany and wresting her from French influence and friendship. *Siegfried* was directed to maintaining the Franco-German alliance, and of the first version, *Siegfried et le Limousin*, Giraudoux wrote, "it is a little pamphlet which I have written to draw to the attention of a certain French public the necessity of rebuilding our ties with literary Germany."[8] The play had the same political intentions.

Giraudoux correctly forecast Germany's direction toward mechanism, Prussianism, and eventually fascism. "Zelten had defects, superb and showy," he had written in the novel, "those with which we have decorated Germans since 1870, but really we must find another nation to wear them now if Germans insist upon becoming bold, rapacious, and practical."[9] While Siegfried displays a liberal rationality, the extremists who back him engage in tautological pretense. "War is the nation!" cries Ledinger. "War is peace!" cries Waldorf. "War is War!" cries Fontgeloy (II:4). The organization of military power behind such false intellectuality, coupled with a passion for homogeneity, leads obviously to fascism, and Germany, as Forestier had said, "instead of following its instincts and the counsel of its past, has been persuaded by its pedants and megalomaniac princes that it must become gigantic and superhuman" (II:2).

Events certainly proved Giraudoux correct in his analysis, and the seriousness of his concern is evidenced in this statement to the American Club of Paris twelve years later, after the war had finally returned:

Everyone is exiled from Germany. All who love music, honest work, and learning are exiled from Germany. We who love Goethe and Dürer—we too are exiled from Germany. . . . It is for all men . . . to reinstate Germany in her true functions . . . to restore to each German his truer self.[10]

This may be presumptive on Giraudoux's part, especially when he adds that "our [French] leaders on the moral plane are those of us who know the real Germany best."[11] Yet Giraudoux is not presenting answers

[8] Frédéric Lefèvre, *Une Heure avec . . .* , p. 150.

[9] *Siegfried et le Limousin*, tr. Louis Willcox, p. 20.

[10] "Réponse à ceux qui nous demandent pourquoi nous faisons la guerre et pourquoi nous ne la faisons pas" (Centre d'Informations Documentaires, 1940), p. 8.

[11] *Ibid.*, p. 9.

to Germany's future, he is simply posing a dialectic. Neither Zelten nor Siegfried holds the key to Germany's future, he maintains, but rather Germany is comprised of the willing cohabitation of both parties. Only when one of them is run out is society endangered. "True Germany" must include both its elements of destiny and humanity, of Bavaria and Prussia, of ancient romanticism and contemporary mechanism. When the balance is destroyed, Germany will become lopsided and will collapse. This again is Giraudoux's dialectical structure: as Woman is defined as the dialectic between Lucile and Paola, Ondine and Bertha, so Germany is defined as the dialectic between Zelten and Siegfried, and neither element may be suppressed. The future of Germany is clearly defined in *Siegfried*; Zelten is exiled and Siegfried departs. The country is left to the fascists.

The panorama of *Siegfried* is political. Germany is split into its two factions and analyzed accordingly; so, in a more limited way, is France. France is detailed as the dialectic between its poetic soulfulness, illustrated by Geneviève and Jacques Forestier, and its rational, bureaucratic humanism, illustrated by Robineau and the customs officer. Robineau is much like Giraudoux himself, a grammarian, an intellectual, a diplomat; a man accommodated to the workaday world with gentle humanism and warm irony. Europe, in the larger picture, is described as the dialectic between Germany and France, or, as Geneviève says, "I never suspected that the wars between France and Germany were civil wars" (II:3).

But although the panorama is social and political, the drama is ultimately personal; a *déchirement* of the soul by the dialectical forces around it. France and Germany, Geneviève and Eva, are tearing Forestier from Siegfried; a latter-day *spharagmos* in the drama:

> *Geneviève:* The only relief we could give him [Siegfried] is to engage in our duel outside of him, not inside his body, tearing his soul apart. . . . Let me give you my hand so he won't think he's being torn in half by irreconcilable forces.
> *Eva:* I won't go that far. [III:5]

Not unlike the more directly personal plays, *Siegfried* describes this tearing apart in the soul; the blind, leaderless decisions a man must make; the "perpetual malaise" (III:5) of total aloneness. "How can a blind man choose?" cries Siegfried madly at the end of the third act. In its conclusion the drama tries to answer this question.

The dilemma is existential, properly speaking, and throughout

Giraudoux has predicated his drama on man alienated from God's jurisdiction and thrust onto his own resources. "I find all living beings condemned to a terrible anonymity," says Geneviève. "Their names, surnames, as well as their ranks and titles, these are only artificial, temporary labels which reveal so little, even to themselves!" (II:2). Identity is not written in the stars or in heaven's log book; it is created by man's own action, by what he chooses to declare himself. Siegfried, in being forced to elect between France and Germany, is a man forced to come to grips with his own identity.

In choosing France, Siegfried—and Giraudoux makes this very clear—is not making a moral decision between nations, he is reacting to the psychological make-up of the human being. "Jacques must choose between a magnificent life which isn't his, and a nothingness which is," says Geneviève (III:2) and Giraudoux cautions that we cannot expatriate ourselves from our heritage and our associations. "There is an invisible garment woven about us, a manner of eating, walking, getting to know people: a divine recollection of the tastes, colors, and smells we first knew as a child. This is our true country" (III:5). Siegfried actually has no choice; the "invisible garment" is one we receive unwillingly and unknowingly, and it cannot be shaken off. "My decision was made the day I was born," says Siegfried, announcing his determination to return to France (IV:3). It lies with that world of destiny from which man was rudely "yanked" into adulthood, and to give it up means to lose that touch with the spiritual and beautiful prehuman world. Rather than continue as the synthetic German chancellor, Forestier will return as an unknown but warm-blooded, ordinary Frenchman.

But he is not willing to let "Siegfried" die, and herein Giraudoux emphasizes once again that if France and Germany are antithetical, they are equal on the same plane, and they must be reconciled within the human soul. In his refusal to let "Siegfried" be completely passed over comes the fullest statement of the play's humane theme of reconciliation:

Ledinger: You prefer to live between two shadows?
Siegfried: I prefer to *live*, simply that. Siegfried and Forestier will live side by side. I will carry both names and both destinies that fate has given me, and I will carry them proudly.
  A human life is not a worm that you can cut in two parts and see each half live by itself. There are no existences so contrary, no experiences so opposite that they cannot be reconciled within a single human life.

> For the human heart is the greatest melting pot that has ever been invented. . . . It would be difficult to believe that the human soul, which houses the most contrary virtues and vices, would only refuse to reconcile the word "France" with the word "Germany." I refuse, absolutely refuse to dig this sort of trench inside myself. [IV:3]

This resolution, which sets a pattern for Giraudoux, is not a declaration of victory but a request for a cease-fire. The human soul encompasses many irreconcilable forces and it cannot suppress any of them. In refusing to "dig a trench" inside himself, Forestier-Siegfried accepts both destinies as his own, both identities as his personal self-definition. He is the product of the conflict between the forces within him, just as Germany and France are the products of their internal opposing points of view. In refusing to reject the "German" in him, Forestier echoes the sentiment of Giraudoux himself, who writes that after the war, "I felt, with all the threads that bound me to Berlin, Dresden, and Munich, clipped, disconcerted on my German side; like a dog whose right-side mustache antennae, giving him his second sight and second hearing, had been cut."[12] Forestier-Siegfried will keep his compound name like the dog his moustache; moreover he will not live *between* the two identities but *within* them. Failing to find "a name halfway between Siegfried and Jacques" (III:5), he accepts both and places his faith in the magnitude of the human heart, with its natural ability to mediate among conflicting desires.

We certainly see in this, his first play, the elements which were to distinguish Giraudoux's theater. The complex, many-leveled structure of antitheses, the insistence on breaking abstractions into warring factors, the resolution by compromise and not cure-all, and the use of characters as ideologic counters on both worldly and cosmic planes reappear constantly in the later plays. The serious intellectual concern of the play cannot be overemphasized, for as a German correspondent reported, it was "the first French attempt truly to understand the German soul."[13] Yet for all its seriousness of purpose, the play is whimsical and delightful, and it is this aspect above all that gives such uniqueness to the "*drame Giralducien*" that the French had to invent a unique adjective to describe it.

What is special about this first play and what fails to reappear in the works that follow is its political optimism. The resolution of *Siegfried*,

---

[12] *Siegfried et le Limousin*, tr. Louis Willcox, p. 18. The words are of "Jean," the narrator.

[13] Friedrich Sieburg, "Jean Giraudoux, *Siegfried*, et l'Allemagne," p. 39.

especially as events were to prove, was too facile. The irreconcilable cannot be reconciled, and in doing so at the end of his play, Giraudoux was hoping against hope. This proved futile.

Politically *Siegfried* was quite ahead of its time, as were all the political plays of Giraudoux. Written between 1922 and 1928, it spoke of the "megalomaniac ruler" who was not to take power until 1933, of the coming conflict between nations which was not evident until 1936, and of the desired hope of a common jurisdiction which was not to take place until the Common Market after the war. Significantly, the 1952 revival of the play was the hit of that season, and the wisdom of Giraudoux not only had stood the test of time, it had aged with increasing dignity. But the simple conclusion of cultural reconciliation was not possible when the peoples of the world had not the rational calm and understanding of the author. Despite Giraudoux's insistent neutrality, the French audiences saw in the play what they wanted to: the result was, as the Paris correspondent for the *Frankfurter Zeitung* angrily reported, merely to confirm existing French prejudices against Germany.[14]

Where Giraudoux had succeeded as a dramatist was in giving fleshed out reality to the ironic, existential ideology. His stage characters, aware of their symbolic existence in a larger drama, were solid supports for the verbal dialectic. This fact, which delighted the French audience to the extent that this became one of the great surprise hits of the decade, all the more incited the *Zeitung* reporter's protests, since, "in the novel we heard Giraudoux speaking to us of Munich as Voltaire had spoken of Babylon, ... but when this is put in front of me on the stage, I cannot prevent myself from recalling reality at each instant."[15]

Where he had failed was in forcing a resolution on an irresolvable subject, and, philosophically, denying the eternal conflict between desire and situation which he himself had posited. Perhaps it was a mistaken attempt to win public appeal, this tacking of a "happy ending" onto the irreconcilable human dilemma; certainly it was not the sort of ending he was ever to write again. In his second treatment of the Franco-German problem, seven years later, he relied on the permanence of the struggle and the inevitability of conflict to establish his theme.

[14] *Ibid.*
[15] *Ibid.*

The Trojan War Will Not Take Place

The Trojan War Will Not Take Place is the most singularly brilliant play Giraudoux was to write, and it rephrases the horrible consequences forseen first in *Siegfried* in a significantly advanced literary form. Cast as a mordant satire on the beginnings of the Trojan War, its contemporary relevance at its 1935 premiere was obvious. "Are you making any allusion to contemporary events?" asked the reporter from *Figaro*. Giraudoux replied cryptically, "None whatsoever—except that it is about war and peace."[16] In the situation which dominates the story of the play, armed Greece lies in wait on the other side of the Trojan "Gates of War," and, as the all-knowing Cassandra says, "Destiny is restless" (I:1). In Europe in 1935, Germany lay in wait across the Rhine, across the Maginot line, and methodically increased its preparedness.

The story of *The Trojan War* is simple and complex at the same time. Helen is Paris' lover, and the Greeks are in the harbor demanding her back. Hector, the warrior, looks for peace. Demokos, the poet, seeks war. The issue polarizes around these men. There is a single issue: will the war be avoided? But in the tortuous action of reversals and intellectual intricacies, a delicate network is structured which rivals that of the most advanced electronic circuitry. As in *Siegfried*, the play's concepts can be displayed on an inverted pyramid of antitheses, but in this play Giraudoux deals more completely with abstractions, less with specific realities. Thus, instead of Germany versus France, we see War versus Peace; and instead of defining Germany by its internal dissensions, Giraudoux gives us War as a combination of component but opposite factors: man's greed for destiny and his revulsion from slaughter. Likewise he demonstrates the ironic nature of peace: the contentment of family life, coupled with a consequent acceptance of hypocrisy and dishonor. Without a protagonist in this play, Giraudoux and his audience find *themselves* at the apex of this conflict of equivalent

---

[16] Almaviva, "M. Jean Giraudoux nous dit ce que sera sa pièce."

definitions. As Jacques Guicharnaud has cleverly commented, "The subject of *La Guerre de Troie* is not the arrival of war, but the hesitation of the world between war and peace.[17] But war itself is a hesitation between two forces—and so is peace.

The diagrammatic structure is the same, only the names are different:

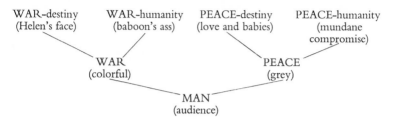

War, a composite abstraction, is seen by its two faces:

Demokos: What does war look like?
Hecuba: Like a baboon's ass. When the female of the species climbs a tree and points her red rear at you, glazed and scaly, surrounded by a filthy wig, that's war you see, that's war's face.
Demokos: With Helen's—that's two faces. [II:5]

Hecuba's version, no less than Demokos', is partial. In the long run of time, war leaves memories of death and ruin; at the moment of its inception, it is a sublime vision of destiny. In *The Trojan War*, the dominant face of war is represented by the absolute and pure beauty of Helen. It is an ethereal beauty as opposed to a voluptuousness; it is clean, precise, mathematical. "She is our barometer, our anemometer," says the geometrician, who pleads for war in her cause. "She is a kind of absolution," says Priam, who refuses to hand her back to Menelaus. She is noncorporeal: a vision, an ideal. "A symbol, you fool!" cried Demokos (II:6). Paris, whose abduction of Helen instigates the play's action, claims that his physical relationship with her is ideally pure, platonic; that "the absence of Helen in her presence is worth everything" (I:4). Thus, incredibly, Helen's war is supported by the intellectuals, the poets, the elders, and the young lovers.

Indeed, the forces which lead to war are seemingly quite pure and noble. They include not only Helen's beauty and transcendant sexuality, but truth and honor. Truth is represented in its absolute legalistic form by Busiris, "the greatest living expert on human rights," who,

---

[17] *Modern French Theatre*, p. 31.

when Hector pleads with him to save Troy and negotiate a settlement, replies in the voice of a stubborn nineteenth-century business tycoon, "I have only one thing to give you, the truth" (II: 5). And both gods and human honor join him in demanding that the Greek insult be answered by Trojan warfare:

Peace: What are the men shouting about down at the beaches?
Cassandra: It seems as though their gods have entered the fracas, also their honor.
Peace: Their gods! Their honor!
Cassandra: Oh huh . . . Hey! You're sick! [I: 10]

Against this opposition, sickly Peace has little to offer. Peace is unpoetic, unsymbolic, impure, certainly not abstractly beautiful; colorless and uninteresting. "I can't read the future. But in the future I see that some scenes are colorful, others quite dim. Until now it has been the colorful ones which have actually taken place" (I:9), says Helen. And her insistence on color—an insistence generally shared by man—does not lead to the life of domestic tranquility.

Hector: You will return home on a gray sea, under a gray sun. But we must have peace.
Helen: I can't *see* peace. [I:9]

This, of course, is a familiar plaint of creatures in love with destiny. Lia cried to Jean, "I don't *see* you. I see a window in your shape which overlooks nothingness" (*Sodom and Gomorrah*, I:3). As Jean lacks the vividness of a demonic archangel, so peace lacks the charisma of war. This is bound to cause trouble among spirited souls, for the contrasting vision is irresistible:

Hector: The battle, do you see it?
Helen: Yes.
Hector: And the city collapses and burns, right?
Helen: Yes. Bright red.
Hector: And Paris? You see the corpse of Paris being dragged behind a chariot?
Helen: Ah! Do you think that's Paris? I see what looks like a piece of the dawn, rolling in the dust. [I:9]

"The city . . . Paris . . . rolling in the dust" is the image Giraudoux brings home with terrifying implications for his countrymen. The ironic pun of Paris-Pâris, accidently available for the playwright, is exploited with effect.[18] War will happen, and war does indeed happen, because it is the force of a vivid, vainglorious destiny, an easy victor over the colorless world of family happiness and mundane compliance with hypocrisy, the gray world where one takes insults with a shrug and pleasures with an attendant, wry apprisal of mortality.

This is, however, but one-half of the picture. We harken back to Hecuba's definition of war as opposed to Demokos': war as a baboon's ass. The bloodiness of war did not need to be demonstrated to the French theater public; France had lost more than two and a half million in the First World War, and virtually no family had wholly escaped the general disaster. Giraudoux's attack on war is rather an attack on the falsely attractive concerns which demand it; the more subtle barbarisms of impotence, pride, and a man's foolishly courageous inclination toward martyrdom.

Hecuba and Hector pierce this artificial appearance of destiny. "You have well demasked them," says Hecuba to her son, referring to Demokos, Priam, and the old men of Troy, "they want to make war for a woman, that's the manner in which impotents make love" (I:6). When subjected to Hector's unmasking, Helen is discovered to be no beauty, Demokos no poet, Busiris no jurist, Paris and Helen no lovers, and finally, war no colorful escapade. It is the *appearance* of beauty, truth, love, and color that will cause the war, it is the actuality of these presences that will suffer by it. This is one of the horrors of war: it dresses itself in splendid but synthetic armor, which takes on an existence quite apart from the man supposedly inside.

Thus Demokos' poetry is ridiculous:

> Viens sans peur au-devant d'Hector,
> La gloire et l'effoi du Scamandre!
> Tu as raison et lui a tort—
> Car il est dur et tu es tendre. [I:6]

Busiris' treasured "truth" is equally academic and absurd. Declaring that the Greeks, in hoisting their colors *au ramat* instead of *à l'écoutière* (nautical terms, probably imaginary), were guilty of an egregious breach of international law which must not be left unanswered, Busiris

---

[18] *Paris* (the city) and *Pâris* (the man) are not pronounced identically in French, but the allusion was nonetheless as obvious to the Parisian spectators as to the reader. If Christopher Fry was aware of this double entendre in the text, he chose to ignore it in his translation (which is generally a fine one), using "his body" for "le cadavre de Pâris," and "flash of sunlight" for "*morceau d'aurore*," the one translation eliminating half of the double meaning, the other removing one of Giraudoux's most important symbols: the dawn.

claims to stand for an absolute standard of justice, irrespective of practical considerations:

Busiris: A warship, my friends, hoists its colors *au ramat* only in response to a salute from a cattle-ship. At the approach to a city and its population, it is therefore the worst kind of insult. There is a precedent. Last year the Greeks hoisted their colors *au ramat* in entering the port of Orphea. The response was immediate. Orphea declared war.

Hector: And what happened?

Busiris: Orphea lost. There is no longer an Orphea, nor Orpheans.

Hector: Perfect.

Busiris: But the annihilation of a nation does nothing to lessen their international moral position. [II: 5]

This is more than inane, it is immoral as well, since the absolute standard to which Busiris refers is nonexistent. Threatened with imprisonment by Hector unless he can "find us a truth," Busiris is all too able to reinterpret the same schedule of "absolute" facts.

Busiris: These are, clearly, alternatives.

Hector: I was sure of it.

Busiris: For instance, couldn't it be interpreted, in certain seas which border on fertile lands, that this salute reserved for cattle-ships is a tribute from the sea to agriculture ... without even considering that the cargo of cattle could be a cargo of bulls? The tribute in that case would even be considered touching on flattery.

Such is the sophistry of demagogues.

The wrongly idealized appearances of love and beauty, like Demokos' bad poetry, are also "sisters of war" (I: 6). Helen is synthetic; Helen and Paris are, in Andromache's words, "a theoretical couple" (II: 8). "They are the symbol of love. They don't even have to love any more," says Cassandra (I: 6). At the end of the play Helen is in Troilus' arms, and the love affair which instigates the Trojan War has ended before the war begins. Ultimately, of course, war is not colorful. Quite the contrary, it is a dismal combat of drab troops sloshing about in the mud under a gray sky. As Hector says in his brilliantly ironic *tirade*, the "discourse to the dead," "war seems to me the most sordid and hypocritical way of making men equal" (II: 5). The prolonged trench warfare, which Giraudoux remembered from Alsace, bore little relation to the glorious battle charges so beloved of poets who had never seen a battlefield. For good reason Hector brings back an army which "hates war"; they, like Hecuba, have seen it. Moreover, Peace is not so colorless as a first glance would indicate. Hector carries her "weights" to Ulysses as his contribution to the scale, which will determine if there is to be war or peace: "my weights are a young man, a young woman, a child to be born . . . the joy of life, confidence in life, the *élan* toward what is just and natural" (II:13). This is a constant vision of the pure, natural harmony which Giraudoux more frequently sought in his fantasies. And Hector and Andromache are *real* lovers, lovers in flesh and blood, lovers so human that they have found, as Andromache admits, that "the life of two people who love each other is an eternal, coldblooded battle with failure. The mark of true couples is the same as false ones: original discord" (II:8). This is not idealized, it is actual. It is the same vision of love as in *Sodom and Gomorrah*.

Ulysses' scales in *The Trojan War* are not well balanced. Emotionally, Giraudoux has allowed us to empathize with peace; intellectually he makes us realize the powerful forces which, once afoot, inevitably lead to war. The desire for peace is a subtle one, appreciable only by experienced and mature sensibilities. The appeal of war is a lie, but a bold and charismatic lie. "At the approach of war every being secretes a new sister, every event dresses in a new veneer: *lies*. Everyone lies. Old men don't love beauty, they love themselves, they love ugliness," says Andromache (II:8). The full realization of the nature of this lie is Hector's. In him the forces of war and peace have long been burning, and the fire never completely dies. He admits that he has, in times past, "allowed himself to be seduced by the little delegation which the gods send you the instant of attack" (I:3). Then:

Andromache: Aha! You feel like a god at that instant?

Hector: More often less than a man. But sometimes, certain mornings, you get up under a different sky. . . . Your body, your arms, they don't weigh the same, they have a different composition. You are invulnerable. A tenderness invades you, you sink into it, a kind of battle tenderness: you are tender because you are pitiless; this must in fact be the tenderness of the gods. [I:3]

A legitimate feeling, to be sure. Giraudoux had written sensitively of his own ambiguous love for war as early as 1919, apostrophizing it in the familiar second person: "Guerre, tu es finie,"[19] and asking himself, "Was I in love with war? Already I was inflexible . . . already I was their [my parents'] elder, I was closer to death than they were . . .

[19] *Adieu à la guerre* (Paris, 1919), p. 7.

already I was pitiless and tender at the same time."[20] The lure of war has, from time to time, appealed to all mankind. But the lure is a lie. Hector continues,

> I think that I hate war—since I no longer love it, . . . You know what it is when you discover that a good friend is a liar? Everything he says after that rings false, even the true things. It seems strange to say—but war once had promised me goodness, generosity—and an end to all baseness . . . the whole gamut of war made me believe in its nobleness . . . it had sounded so just, so marvelously just.

Andromache: And war rang false, this time?

Hector: Why did it happen? Was it because I was too old? Was it simply that fatigue inherent in the trade . . . which overwhelmed me one morning as I was about to finish off one of the enemy, a man about my age. Once the men I killed seemed my opposites. This time it was like kneeling over a mirror. This death I was handing out was a little suicide. . . . From that moment, nothing has sounded right. The spear clanging against my shield, the soldiers falling dead to the earth, the final crumbling of the palaces—it all has rung false.

Hector's response to war is the awareness of the brotherhood of man, and that in taking any life, one is taking a small part of one's own. This, to the French Germanophile Giraudoux, was more than merely theoretical humanitarianism. Death is the irremedial sin. Giraudoux was to defend the "phony war" of late 1939 and early 1940 (when France and Germany bombarded each other with leaflets, not bombs) by saying "We should be disloyal to ourselves were we to sacrifice a single man to the spectacular appeal of war."[21] War is an easy trap for the office-bound bureaucrat, the literary romanticist, the bold or frightened leader to fall into. The situation is two-sided, and its appeal a hard one to resist. Giraudoux's epigraph for *Adorable Clio* (a series of war essays published in 1920) illustrates the ambiguity of a romantic humanitarian: "Forgive me, O war, for having, as often as I could, caressed you."[22]

Giraudoux presents us with a growth pattern, encouraging us to feel that man grows away from war as he experiences it more fully. Those in the play who hate war, it is continually affirmed, are those who know it best. Those who love war and who worship inflammatory symbols are those whose eyesight is impaired by the twin impotencies: immaturity and senility.

---

[20] *Ibid.*, pp. 11–12.
[21] "Réponse à ceux qui nous demandent pourquoi nous faisons la guerre et pourquoi nous ne la faisons pas," p. 6.
[22] In *Œuvres littéraires diverses*, p. 189.

Priam: It must have happened to you, Hector, that a woman
  appeared who was not only a woman but a combination of ideas and
  feelings, which burst from her flesh.
Demokos: As a ruby personifies blood.
Hector: Not for those who have seen blood. I've just come back from
  taking it.
Demokos: A symbol, you fool! You're a warrior, you must understand
  symbolism! You must have met women who, from the moment
  you see them at a distance, seem to you to personify intelligence,
  harmony, sweetness?
Hector: I have seen them.
Demokos: Then what did you do?
Hector: I came near them, and that finished that. [I:6]

A ruby can symbolize blood for those who are not directly aware of
blood. A woman at a distance can symbolize all sorts of promises;
close up she becomes a woman. The symbol is an intellectual distillation;
it can burn with an image of truth, it can stimulate an action, but it
cannot bear close examination from the point of view of detailed
reality. It may even reverse reality, and in the paradoxical world of
The Trojan War, this has become the case. Under the mask of beauty,
Helen is its opposite. "Beauty is the vilest tyrant in the world. It is the
mask that we put over our servility," says Hector in an earlier variant
of the play.[23] Under the mask of truth, Busiris is a finagler. Close
examination, experience, thoughtfulness: these are the enemies of the
symbol and of the rallying cry. Who has more experience with war
than an army, and who hates war more? Understanding, Nietzsche had
discovered, precludes action, and Giraudoux would add that experience is the best preventive of war. Unhappily, narrow-minded
sloganeering can incite one.

Siegfried was offered a choice. In *The Trojan War* there is none. In
Siegfried Giraudoux holds out the frail hope that Germany and France
can be reconciled within a single human soul. In *The Trojan War* peace
and war coexist but unreconciled and unreconcilable. In the jostling
about of two ideas of war and two more of peace, there is an over-
bearing pessimism, a sentiment that there is nothing to be done but let
the war take its inevitable course. "The Universe wants something,"
says Andromache (II:8), and the conflicting desires of man are mani-
pulated toward polarization and war by unseen forces. Using the
Greek framework as a reflection of man's subservience to careless

[23] "Fragments inédits de *La Guerre de Troie*," *Théâtre complet*, 14 (Variantes III): 24.

deities, Giradoux paints the inevitability of war as an insignificant by-product of a heavenly squabble. As the god's messenger explains to the Trojans:

Iris: Aphrodite demanded that I tell you that love is the law of the world . . . she forbids you two, Hector and Ulysses, to separate Paris and Helen. Or there will be war.

Hector: Any message from Pallas Athene?

Iris: Oh yes, Pallas Athene demanded that I tell you that reason is the law of the world . . . and she orders you two, Hector and Ulysses, to separate Helen from the curly-bearded Paris. Or there will be war. [II:12]

Trapped between two conflicting orders from independent and antagonistic goddesses, each promising vengeance if her will is not effected, man finds little solace. There will be war, nevertheless, and the dialectical dilemma of Aeschylus' Orestes is recalled: he is damned if he does and damned if he does not. There is not, however, a higher authority. Orestes had recourse to a court of law (significantly this led to a tied vote), but Priam's appeal to Zeus, "the master of the Gods," leads to the following ambiguity:

Priam: It is neither Aphrodite nor Pallas Athene who rules the Universe. What does Zeus command?

Iris: Zeus, the master of the gods, says that those who only see love in the world are as stupid as those who don't see love at all. Wisdom, Zeus says, is sometimes to make love and sometimes not to make love. . . . He therefore directs Hector and Ulysses to separate Helen and Paris completely by not separating them. [II:12]

As in Aeschylus' Aeropagetica, Zeus has laid down a split decision, a tied vote. An appeal to authority is an absurd one; the answer will be either one-sided or vapidly ambiguous. The synthesis of one manifest destiny and another is simply war to the death.

"It is not in maneuvering children about that one determines destiny," says Helen, "It is not a matter of subleties and trifles. It is one of monsters and pyramids" (I:9). Grave, mystic, archetypal forces are awake in Giraudoux's Troy as much as Sophocles' sphinxed Thebes, and the brutally wise Ulysses speaks all too well of the helplessness of man in the face of such a heavenly onslaught:

Ulysses: The universe knows it, we are going to fight.

Hector: The universe may be wrong. . . .

Ulysses: Let's hope. But when destiny has raised two nations for some years, when it has opened to each the same future of invention and omnipotence; when it has made for each, as we saw a little while back on the scale, a unique and different weighting for pleasure, conscience, and even nature; when it made their architects, their poets, their painters create opposing kingdoms of spaces, sounds, and nuances; when it made the Trojan frame roof and the Theban arch, the Phrygian red and the Greek blue, the universe well knew that it was not intending to prepare two separate paths for mankind to flourish in, but was preparing its festival, the unleashing of the brutality and human folly which alone can satisfy the gods. [II: 13]

It is the prelude to this macabre festival that Giradoux treats, a prolegomenon to future wars. The year 1935, when this play was premiered in Paris, saw Hitler and Mussolini the self-declared men of destiny in Europe. Ethiopia flew the fascist flag, and the attempted German *Anschluss* with Austria had left that country jittery. The shouts of storm troopers parading at Nuremberg drifted insistently over the French border and caused ulcers in Parisian cafés and offices. The battle Giraudoux had forecast was as inevitable and as cataclysmic as the final meeting of matter with antimatter, "opposing kingdoms of spaces, sounds, and nuances," which were not made to live happily side by side. Well could Giraudoux compare Germany to a "restless tiger," for her sounds, demonstrated in *Mein Kampf* and in the Nazi marching songs, were bestial roars which, to the Frenchman's ear, were saying, "Destroy France."

Siegfried was originally written (as a novel) in 1922, and even when the play premiered in 1928, the thought of a second world war was still a remote one in the public consciousness. Yet *Siegfried*, under its wise irony, is presented as a last appeal for compromise and peace between France and Germany. *The Trojan War* was premiered in 1935, four years before the outbreak of the actual conflict, yet at the end of the play the Gates of War open and the struggle begins. This is more than happenstance prophecy; it indicates the presence of an analytical mind which had discovered the vital patterns of behavior at all levels of politics and society, and made informed conclusions regarding the future. By 1935, Giraudoux had discovered the all but inevitable course of events which was to lead to war, and this is his subject in *The Trojan War*.

As with *Siegfried*, the broad political panorama prevents the drama from wallowing in seriousness. Giraudoux delighted in wit, wordplay, and theatrical legerdemain as before—concluding the play with an extraordinary device in which the curtain begins to fall and then rises again. The theatricalism enforces an objectivity over the crucial issue of war, and prevents the play from rigidly taking a side and becoming propagandistic instead of analytic, which it remains. But to indicate his objectivity is in no way to disparage his moral commitment, or to suggest that he watched the coming holocaust dispassionately. The hope remaining in *The Trojan War* is, admittedly, for a miracle (that Helen and Paris can be separated by not being separated), but it is a fervent hope nonetheless, and a clarion call to the future of civilization. It is a hope that man can avoid the "spectacular appeal of war" by realizing the shallowness of the spectacle, by piercing the falseness of the inflammatory jingoists, by recognizing the more truly colorful happiness of family life and home cooking and raising babies. It is by understanding alone that this could come about, and although Giraudoux has thrown in the sponge for his own generation, there will be another, and the new can stand on the shoulders of the old.

The Trojan War is a play about war and against it. It is not mere pacifism—an oversimplification which Giraudoux would have abhorred, and it is far from one-sided. But the message is clear, and when the brilliance of the dialogue, the theatricalism of the setting, and the complex progression of the plot have receded in our minds, the bitterness at war's irrationality remains. Easily comprehensible in its major theme, *The Trojan War* is Giraudoux's final despairing cry for peace, and it has become one of the rare masterpieces of the century. This becomes particularly striking when we see that he followed it, in 1937, with *Electra*, which concludes with an equally passionate cry for war. In the overall dialectic between destiny (war) and humanity (peace), Giraudoux now found himself in the opposite camp. It was a complete capitulation.

Electra

Electra is the third play in the political series, and it is by far the least popular and the least known. Yet P.-A. Touchard claimed it "the last chance for tragedy in the mid-twentieth century,"[24] and, Eric Bentley

[24] *Encyclopédie du théâtre contemporain* (Paris: Publications de France, 1957), Vol. III, p. 124.

considered it worth inclusion in the first volume of his *The Modern Theatre*.[25] Its similarity to *The Trojan War* is obvious: in each play a young girl, acting in the name of destiny, leads her country into a war which means total destruction. In both cases she is opposed by a man who tries to achieve a rational though pragmatic peace. The difference between the two plays, thematically, is simply that in the first we sympathize with the man, and in the second with the girl. And that, naturally, makes an enormous difference.

This play was the third that Giraudoux had based on a Greek legend, but the first that had antecedents in Greek drama. All three classic tragedians had dramatized the tale of the house of Atreus, the royal family of Argos, relating the story first told anecdotally by Homer: the return of Agammemnon from the war in Troy; his murder at the hands of his wife and her lover, Clytemnestra and Aegisthus; their murder at the hands of Agammemnon's children, Orestes and Electra; and the final onslaught of the Eumenides, who threaten the future of the avenging children. Great dissimilarities mark the different versions. Aeschylus made positive what Homer had left ambiguous: the fact that Orestes kills his mother as well as Aegisthus,[26] and that Clytemnestra had assisted in the murder of Agammemnon. He also introduced Electra and the Eumenides into Homer's more skeletal story, and had Orestes "tried" for the murder of his mother. Sophocles, writing some forty-five years afterward, revised the moral implications of matricide by eliminating Aeschylus' Eumenides and the trial of Orestes. Writing of the final vengeance in heroic terms, Sophocles elevated Electra to a dominant position in the planning and execution of the vengeance and made her the title character for the first time.

It is the fourth version of the story, however, the *Electra* of Euripides,[27] that inspired Giraudoux's rendition. Euripides had added two distinctly modern elements to the legend: a psychological analysis of the characters and an ethical dilemma in the plot. Regarding the one, he had liberally spiced the action with discussions of sexual failure, promiscuity, neurotic complexes, tendencies toward incest, and adolescent *Angst*. Regarding the other, he eliminated the Homeric and

[25] New York: Doubleday, 1955.

[26] In *The Libation Bearers*, Homer only says that Orestes killed Aegisthus and then, "when Orestes had done the deed, he invited his friends to a funeral banquet for the mother he had loathed, and the craven Aegisthus." *The Odyssey*, III, tr. E. V. Rieu (Baltimore, 1946), p. 58.

[27] It is convenient to think of Euripides' as the later play, although the evidence is not clear on this point. Both *Electras* were written in or about 413 B.C. Aeschylus' *Orestia* was performed in 458 B.C.

Sophoclean heroism of the children, as well as the shallow villainny of the adults; he made Clytemnestra and Aegisthus into God-fearing, respectable, and bourgeois rulers, and Electra and Orestes into psychotic, lustful, demented adolescents. Euripides' "execution" of Clytemnestra and Aegisthus is a cruel bloodbath, as contrasted to the clean dispatches described by the earlier playwrights, and the moral values which had been suggested earlier were no longer as pertinent.

What remains to condemn Aegisthus and Clytemnestra in Euripides' play is simply one nagging fact: their guilt. Reeking through their humble exteriors is the unsuppressible fact that they have achieved their present positions by regicide. The ethical question that Euripides has posed is this: can guilt be assuaged by rehabilitation? Can a murderer be forgiven if he is now honest, harmless, and virtuous? Should a murder go unpunished if the long-range results have been beneficial and punishment would now be ruinous? Euripides asks these questions but ducks out from under the answers, ending his play with a conventionally ambiguous *deus ex machina*. Giraudoux is one of two modern playwrights to step into the foray. Eugene O'Neill, in his naturalistic trilogy, *Mourning Becomes Electra*, attempts to capitalize on the psychological aberrations that Euripides drew; Giraudoux took for his subject the ethical dilemma. His central theme is justice: should it or should it not be followed to its final conclusion, regardless of circumstance? Although Giraudoux retained the setting and the names from the ancient tale (O'Neill did not), his is the least indebted to classical sources. In no way did he try to recapture the human and dramatic magnitude of the classic versions; rather, he forged an ideological battle between truth and justice on one hand, and happiness on the other. As Giraudoux told Andre Warnod:

Let's simply admit that I have dusted off the statue of Electra, and that I have made her appear as a girl who isn't afraid of making trouble. . . . Electra, for me, is above all a very pure young girl filled with joy and honor, and who accepts none of it, being devoted to finding out the truth about her father's death. The thesis of my play is this: that humanity, by its ability to forget, and by a fear of complications, absorbs great crimes against it. But in every epoch surge forth these pure beings who don't want the crimes to be absorbed, and who prevent that absorption and call a halt to these means which only provoke more crimes and new disasters. Electra is one of these beings. She attains her goal, but at the price of horrible catastrophes.[28]

This thesis supersedes all plot and all tradition.

[28] Warnod, "J'ai épousseté le buste d'Electre, nous dit M. Jean Giraudoux."

For a chorus, Giraudoux presents us with three, a beggar (played by Jouvet), a gardener, and three little-girl Eumenides, who grow up during the course of the play. To add some variety to the story, he has introduced a subplot between the president of the judiciary and his wife, Agatha; a subplot which directly parallels, on the domestic level, the ideological battle fought between the principals. "How nice! A little scandal inside a big one!" says the president ironically. "It's the squirrel in his endless wheel. It gives it the right rhythm," says the all-knowing beggar (II:6). For action, Giraudoux has fashioned an arbitrary and unmotivated sequence of events, which, in a lesser play, would be completely indefensible. He has completely revised the Euripidean version, retaining only the fact of Clytemnestra's and Aegisthus' guilt, and the concluding vengeance of Orestes. Between beginning and end, all is different. The handsome, brilliant Aegisthus rules Argos as regent, and gentle Clytemnestra reigns as queen—they are not married. It has been a prosperous rule; "prices are low, storms pass over our vineyards, heresies avoid our temples, foot-and-mouth disease stays away from the stables," brags Aegisthus (I:3). Electra is discontent, but she cannot tell why. When the play begins, Aegisthus is having her married to a gardener (the character comes from Euripides) in order to settle the last, lingering unpleasantness in the Agammemnon affair. It is at this point that Orestes arrives, and shortly thereafter that Electra discovers, in a vision ("the gift of night"), that Clytemnestra and Aegisthus have murdered her father. It is an inopportune time. Shortly it is announced that the Corinthians have invaded Argos, and that "already the suburbs are burning" (II:7). Aegisthus' obvious course is to marry Clytemnestra, assume the kingship, take control of the guard, and save the city. But here Electra, with her new knowledge, intervenes. Electra must be persuaded not to demand immediate justice if the city is to be saved, for Aegisthus seemingly cannot win the support of the army without her. But this Electra refuses, on the grounds that Aegisthus is a murderer, and "only one with pure hands has the right to save the country" (II:7). To Electra, Aegisthus remains a criminal. Although he may become regent, statesman, husband, king, and "summit of honor" in Argos, still "the gods cannot change a criminal into an honest man" (II:8). On this collision course, the dialectic is waged.

Giraudoux's *Electra* posits in Argos the same situation as that of Troy in *The Trojan War* (and Paris in 1940): a city on the verge of besiegement, struggling to find a proper response to the external threat. Unlike the previous play, however, the Argive struggle is entirely internal; there is no dialogue with the enemy. The play examines its theme from the point of view expressed but not explored by Zelten, "Countries are like fruits, the worms are always on the inside" (*Siegfried*, I:6). In *Electra* Giraudoux dispenses with his attempt to understand Germany and seeks simply to understand France.

The internal struggle is between two polar ideologies: *justice intégrale* versus *justice humaine*. Electra represents the former: an absolutist persistence to root out truth regardless of consequence. Aegisthus represents the latter: a pragmatic realization of the hypocrisy of the world, and a willingness to accept it in return for domestic happiness. Between these two poles lies the vast realm of human behavior, marked by subtlety and infinite variation. Structurally, Giraudoux has located Orestes at the focal point of the two warring ideologies; actually, however, he has the Eumenides bind him and put him in prison for the duration of the climactic scene, so that the audience assumes the protagonist's position and is forced to reconcile the rival points of view. Perhaps more than any of Giraudoux's other plays, this is one that focuses the audience's attention on a moral decision.

Electra is a *jeune fille* with a vengeance, a girl of destiny, a close resemblance to Helen in *The Trojan War*. Like Helen she is young, beautiful ("the most beautiful girl in Argos," says the gardener, I:2), and intelligent. She also shares with Helen the purity of the divine, that quality of being "absent in her presence." "Electra is never more absent than from the place where she is," says her mother (I:4). She is the abstract incarnation of memory and absolute justice (I:2), born of the family of Medea and Phaedra (I:8). Above all she is truth:

> She is truth without residue, an oil lamp without smoke, the candle without a wick. She is the kind who, if she kills all peace and happiness around her, does it because she's right! It's as if the soul of this young girl felt a moment of anguish in the brightest sunlight—as if she sniffed, in the middle of the most splendid festivals and centuries, a leaking of poisonous gas, and she had to go after it until the world cracked and crumbled to its very foundations and its generations of generations, and until thousands of innocents have died an innocent death so that the guilty will live a guilty life. [I:13]

This quest for truth, even to the destruction of the world, is reminiscent of Dr. Stockmann's in Ibsen's *An Enemy of the People*, but Giraudoux carries Electra's search far beyond the narrow bounds of realism. She is totally heedless of practical necessities and scornful of human happiness. "She is going to poison everything with her venom," say the Eumenides, "with her venom of truth, the only one without an antidote" (II:3). Her poison is passive, however, for Electra acts merely by being a witness to a man's degeneracy. "She does nothing. She says nothing. But she is there," says the president, adding that "whenever I see Electra, I feel knocking about inside me all the sins I committed in my cradle" (I:2).

Electra is hardly winsome, and her appearance in the worldly scene is no less destructive than Helen's. The President, with brittle irony, expresses the subtle hypocrisies that are necessary in the world of humanity:

> I know Electra. Let's admit that she is what you say, justice, generosity, duty. But it is by justice, generosity, and duty that the country, the individual, and the best families are brought to ruin. . . .
>
> Because these three virtues contain the only element truly fatal to humanity: implacability. Happiness never comes to the implacable. A happy family means a local surrender. A happy epoch means unanimous capitulation. [I:2]

Happiness is the president's goal, a short-run happiness in his professional, social, and marital life. The Giraudoux happiness must not be thought of as ecstasy; it is quite the opposite. It is a forced reconciliation with the leash. It is maintained by an elaborate network of "adult" adjustments to life, adjustments which salve the symptoms without touching the wounds. Among the most effective is the law: *justice humaine:*

> On our sins, our omissions, our crimes, on truth itself, is daily piled a triple bed of earth, which shuts off the stink: forgetfulness, death, and human justice. It is madness not to let it go at that. It is horrible to think of a country haunted by the ghosts of the murdered, and of them returning from the grave to avenge their wrongs. After proper legal redress, the sleep of the guilty should be as sound as that of the innocents. [I:2]

This "triple bed of earth" is, it is argued, indispensable to life. "All the evil in the world comes from those self-declared purists who want to unearth secrets and place them out in the open," cries Clytemnestra (II:4). Electra, in persisting on her hunt for the truth, is a madwoman

(II:8). She is a "troublemaker," says the president. She is "pious," says the beggar.

Electra is the sum of these adjectives, but she most closely defines herself in the final scene with Aegisthus, wherein the battle for Argos' future is fought. Aegisthus is one of Giradoux's grandest creations: a demonic ruler with great political genius. His policy is to keep the gods out of domestic affairs and not to call attention to himself. "In my city I have warred without mercy against the fanatics who want to signal the gods," he says (I:3), and to do this he marries off the "dreamers, painters, philosophers, suicides, and chemists," or disposes of them in equally silent manners (I:3). He does not exile his enemies, he kills them, and he takes care to do it at night, in the valleys, where no one will notice. His goal is to "keep the promontories vacant and the fairgrounds full" (I:3), and his success in providing bread and circuses to his citizens insures that the messy "Agammemnon affair" will soon be completely obliterated from the public conscience.

The conflict between Aegisthus, with his *justice humaine*, and Electra, with her *justice intégrale*, is beyond compromise. The two come from utterly different worlds. When Aegisthus claims to have been given Argos to rule, Electra claims that she was given the universe.

Electra: Argos is only a point in that universe, my country only a village in that country. . . . And this morning, at dawn, when you were given Argos and its narrow borders, I saw how immense my country was, and I heard its name, a name that you can't pronounce, but which is tenderness and justice at the same time. [II:8]

The dialectic continues without finding any meeting ground.

Aegisthus: And this justice makes you burn down your city and condemn your race. . . . Does the justice of Electra consist of redressing every sin, of making every act irreparable?
Electra: Not at all. But when the crime strikes at human dignity, infests a nation, and corrupts its loyalty, there is no forgiveness.
Aegisthus: Do you know what a nation is, Electra?
Electra: When you see an immense face filling the horizon and you look right at it, and you see its clear, pure eyes, then that's a nation.
Aegisthus: You are speaking like a little girl, not like a king. A nation is a huge body which must be ruled and fed.
Electra: I talk like a woman. . . . What is beautiful, when you think of the real nations, are their enormous eyelids of truth.
Aegisthus: There are truths which can kill a nation, Electra.

Electra: There are dead nations whose eyes still shine. I hope that will
    happen in Argos! But since the death of my father, since the happiness
    of our city has become founded in injustice . . . the sky has fallen in on
    us, we are in a cave where our eyes are useless. Our children are born
    blind.
Aegisthus: A scandal will only worsen this.
Electra: Possibly. But I don't want to see that dull, feeble look in our eyes.
Aegisthus: That will cost millions of glazed eyes, extinguished eyes.
Electra: That's the price. It isn't too much. [II:8]

The dialogue could go on forever. As the beggar says earlier, "They
are both acting in complete good faith. That's what truth is" (I:4).

As in *The Trojan War*, the only synthesis available when destiny and
humanity run headlong into each other is war; total annihilation. At
the play's end Aegisthus and Clytemnestra are killed, clumsily, in the
Euripidean manner. The palace is on fire, the capital is overrun. "It
will be born again," declares Electra (II:10), but the Corinthians are
massacring citizens in the street. "I have my conscience, I have Orestes,
I have justice, I have everything," cries Electra. But how can she sleep
knowing she is guilty of the destruction of Argos, ask the Eumenides.
"I have Orestes, I have justice, I have everything," says Electra. But
Orestes has fled, and will soon be cursing his sister, she is told. "I have
justice, I have everything," says the stubborn Electra (II:10). But is this
really justice, this which causes so much anguish? To conclude the play
a peasant woman, Narses' wife, asks her:

> How do you call it when the day breaks, like today, when everything
> is ruined, sacked and pillaged—although the air still breathes—when
> everything is lost, the city burning, the innocent killing each other—
> but the guilty in anguish . . .

Electra: Ask the beggar. He knows.
Beggar: It has a very beautiful name, Narses' wife. It is called the dawn.
    [II:10]

As in *The Trojan War*, the final verdict is ambiguous, for this will be
a dawn of awesome proportions and chaotic results. "War is unleashed
when a nation becomes degenerate and debased, but it devours the few
just and courageous men and leaves the most cowardly," says Aegisthus
early in the play (I:2). Obviously the slaughter is worthwhile to Electra;
but we must still ask if it was to Giraudoux as well.

During the war Giraudoux wrote a series of essays which, though
never finished, were published shortly after his death.[29] In them he

---

[29] *Sans Pouvoirs.*

wrote darkly about the "degeneration of the French character," of the "malaise between Frenchmen and France, where most of us avoid looking our country in the face, from fear of seeing there an avowal of its feebleness."[30] He complained that "our fiscal policy has made life into a money-game with invitations to everybody. It has changed everyone. It has led to . . . the ruin of authority and the rupture of the citizen's feeling of community within the state."[31] Giraudoux attacked the advent of mechanism, of financial expertise, and of an educational system in which "there is a surplus of instruction and a deficit of education."[32] The picture of France before and during the war, of France after *Anschluss* and the "battle" for the Rhineland, was, to Giraudoux, more than distasteful, it was wretched. Ultimately, only war could be the remedy. In his final essay, "The Future of France," Giraudoux postulates the ultimate need for war as a last resort, to prevent the onrush of mechanism and Prussianism.

In his work as well as in his leisure man used to follow the rhythm of universal life. In fact, man used to be at home on earth. He no longer is. Every day the mechanical tyranny reduces his brotherhood and his communion, of both tastes and interests, with nature. Mechanism is the scalpel that severs the adhesions between twins, between tree and man, animal and man, stone and man.

If the war continues long enough, there will not even be a desire for peace; even for a civilian there will be only an apprehension of peace, for it can bring nothing but the admission from which the war permits us to hide. The admission that the human spirit is no longer responsible, that the human soul lies hopelessly barren, . . . that each man is being watched, like Cain, by a terrible eye whose fixity deprives him of all ease, joy and peace of mind. It is a ritual punishment, which mechanical man was bound to incur by slaying his blood brother.

War is, at the very least, the last means of reviving that slain brother, of reviving courage, imagination, sacrifice, now forgotten, and of reviving them through death. But let's not be mistaken; war risks being the last example of brotherhood—or its last chance—between man and his civilization.[33]

War is not a cure-all, nor is it to be gone into lightly; still war remains the one possibility to revive a degenerate republic, and it is a chance, Giraudoux now insists, worth taking.

While the ideological structure of *Electra* is virtually the same as that of *The Trojan War*, the characterizations have been exactly reversed.

[30] p. 12.
[31] "Les Finances," *Sans Pouvoirs*, p. 64.
[32] "L'Education," *ibid.*, p. 117.
[33] "L'Avenir de France," *ibid.*, pp. 132–34.

Whereas Helen was the superficial shell of destiny and purity, Electra is its incarnation. And Aegisthus, though perhaps wiser than Hector, is, of the two, the more synthetic. Hector would never say, as does Aegisthus, "I believe in the gods. Or rather, I believe I believe in the gods" (I:3).

Aegisthus has no *self*; he is only the sum of his plans. He reacts without a single instinctual or visceral reaction; even his death is impersonal. At the play's end, when he "declares himself," he realizes that he still lacks the central human quality, that which only Electra can give him by anointing him king:

Aegisthus: If I have come to you, Electra, it is because you are the only one
    who can anoint me with the proper oil [*essence*].
Electra: What's that?
Aegisthus: I have the impression that it's something like duty.

Aegisthus, uncommitted to the end, must always be on the defensive. It is Electra's argument which, though it may not win its audience intellectually, must carry the play.

Unlike Helen, Electra is naïvely pure. She is a *jeune fille*, unbounded by adult considerations, quite in harmony with the natural order. Giraudoux emphasizes her spirituality and her kinship with the animal kingdom. "Electra is pious. All the dead are for her," says the gardener (I:2). She "declares herself" at dawn, a time in harmony with the animal world. The beggar urges:

I would hope for morning and truth to begin at the same time. . . .
The truth of men runs too much according to habit . . . 9 AM . . .
6 PM . . . these are bad beginnings. I am accustomed to the manners of
animals. They know how to start something. The first leap of the hare
in the heather at the moment the sun appears, the first jump of the
duck from the blind, the first gallop of the bear from his cave, these,
I assure you are starts toward truth. . . . Be like the animals, Electra,
start at dawn. [II:1]

And she has the support of the "common people," a consideration not irrelevant to the political concerns of Giraudoux. "We are all here, the beggars, the cripples, the blind, the lame, all of us, to save Electra," says the peasant woman at the end of the play (II:9). It seems paradoxical that with Giraudoux, a supreme master of the French language, his purest visions were always the least articulate, and his swineherds, beggars, cripples, and deaf-mutes are his most knowing characters.

The beggar in the play leads these rejects from humanity as a neo-god. "No one has ever seen a beggar as perfectly beggar-like as this one, so rumor has it that he must be a god" (I:3). He has an inside line on the nature of human behavior, unfettered by academic abilities. He readily sees through the evasive political plottings for Electra's marriage and explains with disarming simplicity:

> I have this quality. I don't understand the words of men. I don't have the education for it. I understand men. You want to kill her. [I:3]

The beggar and his fellows are unreconciled to the necessities of compromise and the excesses of hypocrisy. Their actions are harmonious with their true feelings; they will fight to the point of drawing blood over whether a chicken should be cooked with or without the liver, while Aegisthus and his political, rational confreres plot royal assassinations without raising their voices (I:3). Though obviously romanticized, the beggars are the truer realists, and as such, become the vital protagonists of *The Madwoman of Chaillot*. But in this play they support, not supplant, Electra. It is by her efforts that the war is brought on, her total insistence on truth and dedication. It is a hard job for a young girl, which makes the character less appealing than Giraudoux probably had wished, but it is one of the functions of womanhood. Giraudoux considered woman, among other things, as the necessary advocate for purity, honesty, and courage in both public and private life:

> Where men have been asleep, even for five minutes, they reenclose themselves in the armor of happiness: Satisfaction, indifference, generosity, desires. A spot of sunlight reconciles them with incredible amounts of spilled blood, a bird's cry with all kinds of lies. But women are there, all of them, sculpted by insomnia, with jealousy, need, love, memory: with truth. [II:3]

Electra's message may be difficult, even repulsive to accept. But in a world cracking on its foundations, as Giradoux has indicated France was in 1937, it may be the vital medicine.

What *Electra* looks forward to is not so much the advent of World War II, as the Allied liberation in 1944. By 1937, Giradoux suggests, France had reached such a point of immorality and degeneracy that only a wholesale bloodletting could restore it to health. Even if the destruction were nearly total, at least a new dawn might arise, and a new France be reborn. Seen from today's vantage point, Giraudoux's grim hope is exactly what eventually occurred. The foundering

French government of 1937 continued into its bleakest days with the same lack of purpose, lack of initiative, lack of spirituality which Giraudoux decried, and it was succeeded in 1940 with an even blacker collaborationist regime under Marshal Pétain. The totality of war, which saw France overrun by not one but two hostile countries, ravaged by the Allied liberation as well as economically pulverized by four years of Nazi occupation, has somehow led us to a France of the 1960's which is an autonomous power in Europe, perhaps the strongest, most politically vital small country in the world. The "real" Electra, Charles de Gaulle, has consistently and explicitly stood on a program of honor, truth, and *justice intégrale*; and in the 60's France has achieved a prestige she has not enjoyed since Napoleon. "The destiny of France is to be the irritant of the world," proclaimed Giraudoux in *L'Impromptu de Paris* (which immediately followed *Electra* in 1937), and in the era of De Gaulle, an independent, nuclear France has indeed been both a respected and an accursed nation in capitals abroad.

Electra is by far the darkest of the political plays, and its stage history has been spotty. Two plays which have been somewhat modeled on it have had more popular success—Anouilh's *Antigone* and Sartre's *The Flies*. *Antigone* takes the central theme whole (*justice intégrale* versus happiness and conciliation) and Sartre takes the story and his title (Giraudoux calls the Eumenides "flies" in I:1) as well as many of the characterizations and ideas. Giraudoux's theatricalist style of Greek revival stands in uneasy balance with his awesome theme. He embroiders *Electra* with the same devices he used in *Ondine*: plays within the play, music, song, literary and dramatic manipulations, a farcical domestic subplot, even a remarkable *tirade* by the gardener, who leaves the play at the end of the first act and addresses the audience to "explain" what the play is about. The harmony, however, is missing. *Electra* is a madly perverse play, which was written in a madly perverse time; an audience could have shrugged off the "impossible" dialectics of Isabelle and of Siegfried, but it was impossible to shrug off the oncoming rush of World War Two. *Electra* is the ominous frenzy before the storm.

The "dawn" which the beggar proclaims at the end of *Electra* is not to be taken cynically. Its hope is the reason that the play was written. In 1940 Giraudoux wrote:

What is needed is faith, faith in the future. To have that we must regard the peace that is coming not as an end in itself but as a stepping stone to better things. Unlike the peace of 1918, this peace must not mean merely a falling back into the prewar rut. . . . This war, the worst of evils, must be made to serve a purpose: to act as the sluice-gates between a bygone era and a new age.[34]

To Giraudoux the sacrifice was not too much, and in fact it was a sacrifice he made himself. Giraudoux died shortly before Paris was liberated in 1944. But not before leaving his "last will and testament" for the future of France. This was *The Madwoman of Chaillot*.

The Madwoman of Chaillot

It may seem too narrow to speak of *The Madwoman of Chaillot* as the conclusion of this political tetralogy of France in the Second World War. The play is full of fancy, a superbly whimsical collection of farce, fantasy, and flippancy, which has achieved as great a popular success as any of Giraudoux's plays. Social seriousness, which continually peeks from the interior of *Siegfried* and *The Trojan War*, and is mixed with bothersome intellectual discursions in *Electra*, seems at first totally missing from *The Madwoman*. One American textbook edition even bases its approval of the work on its total removal from the current scene: "For some theatregoers . . . the play seemed too remote from the harsh facts of contemporary history, and many wondered how Giraudoux could write so spirited a comedy during a period of national suffering and despair. Plainly, none of the anguish of the existential drama of the French Occupation is present in Giraudoux's extravaganza. . . . The remoteness of the mood and characters from the dark reality of the day is itself part of the play's charm."[35] But this is hardly "plain" and, under examination, is seen to be simply a mistake. Certainly the "anguish of existential drama" is not readily apparent to the theatergoer but it can be found in the very bones of the play.

The Madwoman was completed in 1942, and the script was sent to Jouvet in South America, where the director was leading his troupe on a two-year tour. On the title page Giraudoux had written, "This play

---

[34] *The France of Tomorrow*, p. 5.
[35] Haskell M. Block and Robert B. Shedd, *Masters of Modern Drama* (New York: Random House, 1962), p. 730.

was presented for the first time on the 15th October, 1945, by Louis Jouvet, at the Théâtre de l'Athénée."[36] The prediction was off by only two months and two days, and the splendid Jouvet premiere, subsidized by the state, signaled the postwar rebirth of French theater. As Janet Flanner (Genêt) reported to her American readers in early 1946,

its wildfire popularity, which makes seats almost impossible to buy, is an encouraging sign of revived public intelligence. The piece is already established as probably the most influential success of the modern French theatre. For several days after its première, the play was a topic for the editorial columns of nearly every newspaper in town. In their various emotional and ideological flights, they compositely declared that one felt in the presence of a miracle; that it was a high French moment which the world envies France, the peak of Giralducien art, a lesson which we will never forget, the ghost of Beaumarchais, and an anticipation of the revolution which is coming.[37]

Fittingly, Giraudoux's last play produced under Jouvet's stewardship was, as his first, an inspiring social document, illustrating the length and persistence of Giraudoux's political commitment.

The play divides society into two races, one of eccentrics and the other of pimps. The former is the carry-over from the army of beggars in *Electra*, and one of their leaders, The ragpicker, is the more earthly variant of Electra's beggar; both roles having been first performed by Jouvet. The true leader of this army, however, is the Madwoman Aurélie herself, "A *grande dame*. Silk skirt leading to a train, but gathered up by a metal clothespin. Louis XIII slippers. Marie-Antoinette chapeau. A lorgnette hanging on a chain. A cameo. A basket... a dinner bell in the bosom of her dress" (stage direction, Act I, p. 102[38]). Supporting the mad, fantastical mélange are three more madwomen: Constance, the madwoman of Passy; Josephine, the madwoman of la Concorde; and Gabrielle, the madwoman of Saint-Sulpice; plus a flower girl, a street-singer, a deaf-mute, a lace merchant, a pair of lovers, a sewer king, some historical antivivisectionists, and "the friends of vegetables." The enemy army is the one of *mecs* (pimps) a nameless, faceless assortment of presidents, prospectors, barons, brokers, secretaries general, and petroleum lobbyists. Between these two armies, a comic war is waged, but it must not be forgotten that this war, like its contemporary, is a war to the death.

---

[36] André Beucler, *Les Instants de Giraudoux*, p. 38.

[37] Janet Flanner, *Paris Journal 1944–1965* (New York, Atheneum, 1965), p. 52.

[38] There are no scene divisions in *La Folle de Chaillot*. Page references are to the Grasset edition of Giraudoux's works, vol. 4.

The setting is the Café de l'Alma in the Chaillot district of Paris, and the café represents all which history and culture have deposited in the French capital. "At this same place Molière, Racine, and La Fontaine used to come to drink their wine," says the prospector (I, p. 101), and it had also been the scene of Giraudoux's meetings with Jouvet. The madwoman and her friends are long-time residents of the area; the pimps, we see immediately, are newcomers. And they control everything. They corrupt everything. Their goal is to destroy Paris and retrieve the oil which they have found under the city's innards. As the play begins, the prospector has laid a bomb which he expects will blow up Chaillot. The ragpicker explains, "There's been an invasion, Countess. The world is no longer beautiful, no longer happy, because of the invasion" (I, p. 123). The action of the play is simple: it consists of the madwoman learning of the nature of these "invaders," condemning them *in absentia* in a mock trial, and ridding the world of them by sending them down into a bottomless pit, which the sewer king shows her how to open.

There are three levels of social analogy that are drawn in this colorful adventure, each simultaneously existing as a satiric analysis of the current political scene. On the primary level the play is, in the words of textbook commentators, "a parody of modern finance capitalism,"[39] and the *mecs* are property pimps (the "mackerel pimp," the "white wine pimp,") who attach themselves to various objects of man's need and desire, and succeed in getting a cut on the exchange. As the play begins with their sitting at the Café de l'Alma, arrogantly discussing their schemes to increase their sizable fortunes, they resemble nothing so much as the Parisian black-marketeers, described in this article, which appeared in *France-Europe* about the time *The Madwoman* was written:

M. Nénesse enters a small bar near the Opera. He walks heavily and carelessly on thick, creaking leather soles to his reserved table. The waiters bustle around him. [He adjusts] his gold watch and takes a Chesterfield from his gold cigarette case, which weighs at least 300 grams. . . . Out of a bicycle taxi steps either an important colleague or a client of this 1943 tycoon. The new arrival is of indeterminate age. . . . In the abrupt tones that you used to hear in the underworld, the two men converse. The newcomer tears a corner off the paper tablecloth and writes some mysterious figures on it. It all has to do with "boîtes bleues," "paquets verts," and "douze tonnes de purée." Finally, the fat man pulls a thick wad of 5,000 franc notes out of his inside pocket, and M. Nénesse stuffs them away without batting an eyelid. The phone rings. It's for

---

[39] Block and Shedd, *Masters of Modern Drama*, p. 730.

M. Nénesse. He doesn't bother to go up to the phone booth; he takes the long-distance call downstairs.

"The trucks from Belgium haven't turned up. And the tobacco . . . "

Everyone can hear, but what does it matter? M. Nénesse is outside the law. . . .

Before the war, plain Nénesse was in the white slave trade. After the defeat, Monsieur Nénesse traded in meat, poultry and butter. . . . Every day this honest tradesman sells 300,000 francs' worth of goods and collects a cool fifty percent rake-off.[40]

Nénesse, formerly a real pimp and now a vegetable pimp, exactly resembles the Giraudoux *mecs*, who also sport expensive cigarette lighters (with private-stock cigarettes), arrogant titles, disrespect for authority, distaste for the human beings about them, and a private code-language of financial doubletalk. The president and his friends, like M. Nénesse, exhibit complete freedom from legal prosecution because they control the law; their word is law. "Hundred franc notes belong to the rich, not to the poor," he tells the ragpicker (I, p. 89) as he takes the note away. Money belongs to the pimps; it is their language, and the ragpicker says of them as was said of M. Nénesse, "When they meet they whisper and pass each other fifty-thousand franc notes" (I, p. 124).

The attack on capitalism as pimpery was especially meaningful in France, where not only the black market but an outrageously political system of economic policies had hamstrung the country since the First World War. Giraudoux had complained for many years of the system where money, more and more, had become disassociated with goods, and where the agent of a product became more necessary than its producer. In *Sans Pouvoirs* he wrote, "Our financial policy has become a money game. . . . It has detached money from its real values; and has allowed our great national resources to go to waste by detaching money from work, from function, and even from gold itself."[41] It is this aspect of capitalism which, Giraudoux felt, is unnatural and pernicious; the substitution of a seemingly synthetic system of trade for a natural bartering of intrinsic worths. As an economic grievance, however, this may be merely nostalgia, since Giraudoux did not or could not suggest alternative systems of commerce.

[40] Gerard Walter, *Paris under the Occupation*, tr. Toby White, pp. 101–102.
[41] *"Les Finances,"* p. 64.

The satire against capitalism and economic pimpery is a hollow one, and far from being the principal subject of Giraudoux's interest, it is actually only a sidelight. More crucial to the play's structure is the analogical relationship of the story to the French-German theme from the earlier plays, a theme considerably more deeply buried in the theatrical froth than the other. For by this analogy Giraudoux paints his story of the German occupation of his city: the madwoman and her café friends represent the citizens of Paris (and of France), and the army of pimps represents the German occupying forces. Considerable evidence warrants this comparison, admittedly a surprising one considering the play's tone.

The imagery of the script is entirely that of a nation at war. The pimps are "invaders," their take-over of Paris has been an "invasion," they are of "another race," and they have arrived in their positions as a result of a series of murders:

> Ten years ago, one day, my heart jumped. Among the passersby
> I saw a man with nothing in common with anyone else; stocky stout,
> his right eye rakish, his left anxious, another race. He swaggered, but
> in a funny way, somewhat menacing and uneasy, as if he had killed
> one of my friends to take his place. He *had* killed him. He was just the
> first. The invasion had begun. Since then not a day has passed without
> one of my friends disappearing and one of the new ones replacing
> him. [I: p. 124]

They take the place of murdered Parisians as the German forces took the places of men killed in the hapless attempt to hold back the Wehrmacht. They are the uniform and uniformed army; faceless, nameless, "locked to one another like alpinists on a chain," (I, p. 126). When they appear in the final scene, it is in groups of identical robots who follow each other down the bottomless pit, as armies follow each other into war.

They have completely taken over the administration of Paris. "They run everything. They corrupt everything," says the ragpicker. "The era of slavery has arrived. We are the last free people" (I, p. 125). They have appropriated for themselves the grand châteaux in the Loire valley for their personal residences, and have decorated them with ballet girls from the Opera (II, p. 160). They are not only above the law, they make it into a rapacious and humiliating weapon. They respect neither tradition, culture, nor personal decency; they "bathe naked, if they choose, in the fountains of the Place de la Concorde . . .

they can turn to you their *derrières*, my dear ladies, and you will smile at them and kiss them as you would their faces. You *will* kiss . . ." (II, p. 163). The cruelty of the *mecs* is far more than the cruelty of ordinary capitalists; it is the behavior of a spiteful Nazi empire.

While the German forces were at first kept to fairly rigid standards of conduct during the Occupation, their presence was felt in every corpuscle of the invalided French body. Grey-suited German soldiers mingled almost imperceptibly with Parisians at Auteuil, at the Opera, and in the corner cafés, but the apparent serenity was merely on the surface. One Frenchwoman wrote, "They pass by, two by two, four by four, rarely alone; stiff, grave, hardly talking, . . . without the radiant careless smile of youth, without any of the charming abandon that shows real camaraderie. . . . They no longer are human beings, they are creatures galvanized."[42] Galvanized by fanaticism, to be sure, also by the incredible power which had fallen into their hands. The Germans, like the madwoman's *mecs*, had billeted the great châteaux and turned them into military headquarters. They splashed German highway signs all over Paris, and Parisian nightclubs reverberated to Nazi drinking songs. They were the ones who, in 1942, were buying French girls for their pleasures, swimming nude in the fountains of La Concorde, administering an economy for which they produced nothing, suppressing individual expression and individual belief to the point of committing French citizens to German concentration camps, and, in short, running and corrupting Paris without being Parisian. When the pimps disappear at the end of *The Madwoman* and the flower girl cries out, "The armistice must have been signed" (II, p. 177), it should be obvious what future armistice Giraudoux had then in mind.

Giraudoux does not mention Germany once in the script, and the names of some of the invaders are Duval, Durand, and Boyer; never Schmidt or Ribbentrop or Biedermann. This could possibly be due to an early thought of Giraudoux to produce the play during the Occupation, or it could simply be a measure to maintain the light tone of whimsical fantasy. But there is one precise linkage between the events of the play and of the contemporary situation, and this is the figure of Adolphe Bertaut.

Adolphe is the former lover of the madwoman, and their aborted affair haunts the play. They had courted in the 1890's, "when the Tsar

---

[42] Thomas Kernan, *France on Berlin Time*, p. 147.

entered Paris," but had broken apart years afterward, and Adolphe had married a woman named Georgette, whom he never loved. "That's the way men are," the madwoman explains. "They love you because you are good, spiritual, and transparent, and when they get the chance they leave you for some woman who is ugly, colorless, and opaque" (II, pp. 166–67). Thirty years after that, but still before the play begins, they met again, but that time Adolphe did not recognize his countess Aurélie, and instead he stole a melon from her. Finally, at the end of the play, "all the Adolphe Bertauts of the world" come to return her melon and demand her hand (II, p. 178). But now she refuses. This is the story of Adolphe Bertaut, and it is a puzzling one since it seems at first to have so little relation to the rest of the play.

It could be no accident that this mysterious character has the same name, Adolphe, or Adolf, as the one man whose name virtually personifies the Second World War. In 1942 "Adolphe" could bring thoughts of only one man. Even a hundred years from that date, no parent and no author will be able to use the name "Adolf" innocently. Moreover, Adolphe is a very German name in this French play, and he is described as wearing a "cronstadt" (a German stiff hat) and having a suspicion of a harelip (I, p. 112), which was rumored at the time to be the reason for Hitler's moustache. Through the character of Adolphe Bertaut, Giraudoux shows his own love affair with Germany, his disgust at being jilted in World War One and being stolen from (the melon) at Alsace-Lorraine, and his final and complete repudiation of the German nation in World War Two. Although Siegfried, speaking for Giraudoux, refused to dig a "kind of ditch inside myself"; when the madwoman answers Adolphe's final, post-armistice appeal, it is with words of total rejection: "Too late! Too late!" (II, p. 178):[43]

> *Madwoman:* I say that when they had the 24th of May, 1880, to declare
> themselves, the most beautiful Pentecost Monday that had ever been
> seen in the Varrières woods, or the 5th of September, 1887, when they
> took and grilled a pike for our picnic at Villeneuve-Saint-Georges, or
> even, if necessary, the 21st of August 1897, when the Tsar entered
> Paris, and when they let all these days pass without saying anything
> to you, then it is too late! [II, pp. 178–79]

The cultural bond had never been tied; Germany and France had remained enemies through all opportunities, and had remained

[43] The authorized English translation by Maurice Valency unhappily uses the acting direction "sadly" for this line. Giraudoux says "*criant.*" The line is cried out with sadness, yes, but with rage as well.

unreconciled within the human framework. Speaking from the 1942 vantage, Giraudoux could say nothing else.

Adolphe's story is never told except in sketchy references, and he only appears at the very end of the play. But it is the climactic moment, and the rejection of the Adolphe Bertauts leads directly to the play's concluding statement: "If two beings who love one another let one single minute get between them, it becomes months, years, centuries" (II, p. 179). Reconciliation in 1942 was beyond hope, and the world would have to turn its efforts to the conflicts of the future. The future would learn from the present, and, as in *Electra*, Giraudoux sees beyond the war to the era which will follow. The madwoman turns to the hesitating young lovers and cries to their friends:

> Make them kiss each other, the rest of you, or else in an hour she will be the Madwoman of Alma and he will have a white beard. (*They kiss*). Bravo! If only that had happened thirty years ago, I wouldn't be here today. [II, p. 179]

If France had embraced Germany in 1919, if Giraudoux and others had succeeded in making Frenchmen realize the necessity of rebuilding the ties with Germany, as he had attempted in *Siegfried*,[44] or in making Germans aware and ashamed of their false idol of destiny, as he had attempted in *The Trojan War*, the war would not have taken place. Failing that, the time had already come to begin preventing the wars to follow.

The ending of *The Madwoman of Chaillot* is a total capitulation to theatricalism and a violent attempt to escape, even momentarily, from the dialectic. The ending is an act of genocide which only an extreme degree of stylization makes palatable. It is as though the oppression of three years of Nazi occupation had so burdened Giraudoux that in one enormous, irrational shrug he simply disposed of it through fantasy. The tetralogy of fifteen years' concern over Franco-German relations has ended with an act of irredeemable violence and has relinquished all hope of reconciliation short of mass slaughter.

In this conclusion Giraudoux adheres to the basic thought of *Electra* but with one major difference: *Electra* ends with only the dimmest forecast of what the postwar future would bring, and *The Madwoman of Chaillot* gives us a detailed plan. Thus the enormous difference in tone between the plays; the earlier, prewar play looking futilely at the

---

[44] Frédéric Lefèvre, *Une Heure avec . . .*, p. 150.

immense black tunnel ahead and only seeing the dimmest "dawn" infinitely far away, and *The Madwoman* peering clearly into a postwar future with eagerness and enthusiasm. In terms of sentiment, no two plays could be more different. *Electra* is a forecast of war, *The Madwoman* one of peace. In 1940 Giraudoux told an audience, "Peace must find us with our programme ready, cut and dried down to the last detail."[45] *The Madwoman*, as much as the political essays in *Sans Pouvoirs* and *Pour Une politique urbaine*,[46] became Giraudoux's last will and testament for the future of France, and of European civilization. This is the third, final level of social analogy.

In this light, *The Madwoman* is Giraudoux's warning against the evils of a mechanized, technological society. It is no longer merely Prussianism that concerns him, it is the oppression of technological progress, either American, German, or Russian; the oppression of a technocracy which seeks to devalue individuality, artistry, history, and culture and to insist upon, in their places, efficiency, sterility, neatness, and uniformity. What terrified Giraudoux about this particular war, which was being battled about France's head, was that it led only "to the thought that peace will be no more than a horrible adjustment between a mutilated white race and a triumphant mechanical civilization."[47] It was this thought above all which generated *The Madwoman*, as can be seen in several illustrations.

The pimps are the agents of technological progress; in their faceless anonymity they are the identical pistons in a huge economic machine. Their bent is for progress but their result is destruction. As the madwoman explains:

> Men everywhere who seem to be building are secretly involved in destruction. The newest of their buildings is only the mannequin of a ruin. . . . They build quays and destroy rivers (look at the Seine), build cities and destroy the countryside (look at Pré-aux-clercs), build the Palace of Chaillot and destroy the Trocadéro. . . . The occupation of humanity is only a universal enterprise of demolition. [II, p. 141]

Progress, in the technological society, is merely a change from one form to another, and in the wanton sacrifice of the old, Giraudoux feels, vital components of the human character are destroyed.

[45] *The France of Tomorrow*, p. 5.
[46] Monaco, 1946, and Paris, 1947, respectively.
[47] "L'Avenir de France," p. 134.

The technocrats are "cool" people, bespeaking an age in which emotion gets in the way of expertise. "They don't run, they don't hurry. You never see them sweat," says the ragpicker (I, p. 124). Their motivating source is oil, and their taste for it is sensual, lustful. They find oil under Paris and so will destroy the city to get it. "What do they want to make with it?" asks the madwoman. "What one makes with oil—misery, war, ugliness," answers the young lover (I, p. 122). The interchangeable "presidents of administrative councils, delegate administrators, self-conscious prospectors, contingency stock-brokers, secretaries general of enterprising syndicates, patent expro-priators, . . . publicity arrangers" (I, p. 126), who are the ice-blooded arbiters of technological society, have no use for the queer assortment of characters that frequent the madwoman's café; and the future con-flict, we realize, is to be between these technocrats and the less pro-gress-minded. They will either be absorbed or eliminated. The first method is demonstrated at the play's beginning, where the baron is taken into the fold by the president. The fifty-odd year old baron exemplifies the degenerate French spirit, and his name, Jean Hippolyte, is the exact reversal of Giraudoux's. He has disposed of his inherited French estates for a series of foreign mistresses. "The more French the name of my estate—the more exotic the name of my mistress," he says pathetically (I, p. 88), referring to the falling apart of the French Empire, both physically and spiritually.

But many cannot, or will not be absorbed, and these the invaders must liquidate. The broker summarizes the course of action which must be taken against the madwoman and her friends, and its reasons, in this peroration from an early draft of the play:

> This madwoman . . . that dealer in shoelaces, that juggler, these are our
> real enemies, Mr. Prospector. . . . Those who have a sense of humor,
> a nostalgia for the past (which we abolished!). We others, we pioneers
> of the modern age, we had thought that by the division of the world
> into two classes; one of workers and the other a managerial elite; one
> sweaty and the other perfumed, that by the radical suppression of all
> connections between money and the poor, between leisure and work,
> we thought we would have sterilized the epoch once and for all! The
> diversity of human types has become a major problem for the
> conscientious managerial executive . . . we have been thinking of
> reducing them to a single popular type. A thousand exploitees per one
> exploiter, how convenient that would be, how restful for the conscience.
> But look! Look about this district, which we have filled with the

largest number of delegate administrators in Paris, the district that we want to make the citadel of power and money, . . . see these flesh-and-bone ghosts of liberty. . . . These are the phantoms of joyful poverty, of madness.[48]

This statement, somewhat attenuated in the final version in order to preserve the light tone of the play, gives an ironic rationale for all "clean" economic systems, which gain efficiency by reducing man to a uniform figure, easy to program, easy to monitor, easy to keep in line. Such systems were proposed to France during and after the war, first by Hitler through the Vichy government; afterward by America, via SHAPE, NATO, and European Recovery; and by Russia, via the French Communist Party. All these forces fought for France's destiny in the 1940's and 50's, and not until the present republic under De Gaulle can France truly be said to have taken her destiny into her own hands. Even this, Giraudoux had prophesied. "The only hope rests with De Gaulle,"[49] he had said shortly before his death. While he never was to appreciate the full import of that remark, the relevance of these political concerns became enormous in the postwar period.

The prophesied future for which Giraudoux ultimately hoped was not a sentimentalized fantasy world of madwomen and shoelace peddlers (just as the technocrats were not to be faceless, identical robots —at least in the literal sense), and his rebellion against the mechanized society was considerably more than nostalgic, wistful rumination. He was a political realist, and he had a program. It was not his idea of dramaturgy to use the theater for this sort of exposition; and the play must be seen as a general sounding of alarm rather than a detailed manifesto. Nonetheless, the play offers certain definite guidelines toward the future. It appeals to the Frenchman's love for freedom and to his searching after personal and natural glory. (The president became a pimp only after he had sacrificed his dreams of glory and "turned instead to the inexpressive and nameless faces." [I, p. 89.]) It appeals to a respect for tradition, for history, and for a natural state of man and country. It demands a tolerance for all sorts of eccentricities and peculiarities which define the human being. It celebrates the simple qualities of provincial life, and demands that they be protected in an increasingly urban world. To Giraudoux, born in rural Bellac, this was

48 *Théâtre complet*, 15 (Variantes IV): 37–38.
49 Jean Blanzat, "Giraudoux et la Résistance."

what the war was all about: the preservation of the simple, honest, French way of life. Defending the war, he wrote in 1940:

What sort of man is a Frenchman? He is a man who likes to spend his time not in the glorification of a race, nor in manifestations of some dark divinity within him, but in simple ways of daily life, the ways of living that his forefathers bequeathed him, in a pleasant, fruitful land, a life based on rational principles and respect for the rights of others. He has his rules of conduct: work, activity, a lively interest in all things. He has his pleasures; the joys of family life and the company of friends; his hobbies, such as fishing and bowling. And he has his special passions—a passion for personal freedom ... with which he tolerates no interference, and a passionate dislike of injustice."[50]

Idyllic? Of course. But Giraudoux was never to shrink from an idea merely because it seemed sentimental. Sentiment, he felt, was one of the distinguishing abilities of the human species, and proper sentimentality was consonant with an honest, natural manner of life. The stability of rural life, which was also that of French life, was in Giraudoux's mind a reflection of French rationality—an essential honesty between body and spirit. "I hate ugliness, I adore beauty," says Irma Lambert, the dishwasher (I, p. 130), in words similar to Agatha's in *Electra*. In both cases it is the obvious truth that is shocking to hear said, for it is the truth of the body rather than the politic speech of society. By contrast, progress is, in Giraudoux's thoughts, an unnecessary demand of the "world of humanity," which continually yanks man from his more natural, honest and peace-loving destiny; and mere progress, by itself, must be resisted. "France has always had one principle, one program: to be contented with the existing state of things, and whenever feasible, to turn it to account and to ameliorate it,"[51] said Giraudoux, who craved a society which would slowly evolve by internal movements and august leadership, never by revolution or ideological invasion. Though often thought of as a liberal (as he would probably be called in America), Giraudoux was a staunch conservative. He wished to conserve the trees,[52] conserve the simplicity of rural life, and conserve the importance of love, nostalgia, beauty, and communality. These values are not frequently spoken for in literature, not at least in good literature, for they smack of the obvious and the

---

[50] *Réponse à ceux qui nous demandent pourquoi nous faisons la guerre*, p. 4.

[51] *Ibid.*

[52] A common theme. "A nation finds itself in trouble with destiny ... by its faults ... such as the citizens wantonly cutting down the trees." *Trojan War*, II:13.

oversentimental. Yet Giraudoux laced them with such brilliant measures of irony, wit, and savage understatement that they have become quite palatable.

Peace must bring this freedom to conserve the old while relishing the new, Giraudoux maintained. To the troops fighting for the country, he defined the policy of the war:

> You must look forward to a France equipped for action and well-being on modern lines. While you are defending your country, you must feel assured that, when peace comes, you will find awaiting you not only the heritage of our agelong civilization—which we shall do our best to keep intact for you— but also a larger freedom, a wider field of enterprise, more trustworthy guides and ample safeguards, at last made thoroughly effective against parasites and profiteers.[53]

Giraudoux's activity in establishing the new France "on modern lines" was not strictly limited to polemics. He revived and reorganized the important *Ligue Urbaine et Rurale* and authored its manifestos and policy documents. The league functioned after the liberation and "followed out, on the practical level, the goals which Giraudoux had broadly fixed."[54] He traveled extensively to collect information and spread his gospel—even during the Occupation. He did work in the details as well as the general policies, and worked extensively to preserve certain monuments and parks in the city of Paris in their original forms. It could be argued that this work was trivial, yet that argument is shortsighted. What Giraudoux sought above all for France was a pride in Frenchness, a cultural nationalism, a love, amongst the citizens, of their environment. And no one can now doubt that this pride—or stubbornness as foreigners occasionally consider it—is a major factor in France's international prestige in the postwar world.

For this is the import of *The Madwoman of Chaillot*, and in the 1945 production it came across loud and clear. It was an appeal to Frenchmen not to be swept up in immediate reconstruction and reindustrialization, not to allow any systematized economy to engulf the nation, not to permit France to be left to the mercy of either her enemies or her allies.[55] It is not strictly a matter of capitalism or communism, but of

---

[53] *The France of Tomorrow*, p. 5.

[54] Raoul Dautry, appendix to Jean Giraudoux, *Pour une politique urbaine*, p. 144.

[55] Giraudoux was more afraid of the Allies than of Germany. His last days were spent attempting to create an agency which would tabulate French losses in the war as a negotiating weapon for reparations. He was fearful that the Allies would run the entire peacetime show themselves. See Blanzat, "Giraudoux et la Résistance." p. 2.

"isms" in general. It is an appeal for France to hold on to her eccentricities and irregularities, to protect the individual freedom of her non-conformists, her artists, and her "unproductive" citizens. It is an appeal for the persistence of history and culture, for the maintenance of national monuments, the Trocadéro, the Café de l'Alma, Paris itself and rural quiescence. It is an appeal for France to find her destiny in the values of honesty, simplicity, and purity—rather than in mechanical, technological confusion. In France, these issues are entirely real. Giraudoux's appeals, by and large, have been followed. Once more Giraudoux has been the prophet of the future.

The political tetralogy is probably more important for the vitality of the plays than for the profundity of their ideas. However, the subtle understanding of the Franco-German conflicts and the internal political struggles of France are brought to light by this diplomat-author with continual wisdom and foresight. As mentioned, the 1928 *Siegfried* deals with the mid-1930's, the 1935 *Trojan War* deals with the events of 1939, the 1937 *Electra* is involved with not only the coming of war but the coming of liberation in 1945, and the 1942 *Madwoman of Chaillot* is concerned with the goal of liberation, and beyond that, the urgent problems of a postwar period which Giraudoux was not alive to see. More than the moral and metaphysical plays, the ideas in the social plays had a serious effect on the audiences which were exposed to them, and they were carried farther in strictly social and political documents, which Giraudoux continued to write until his death. They were in part enacted in the day-to-day work of his professional life. He was, of course, a writer only during his vacations, and he considered his writing a fundamental part of his working, thinking life. He considered his literary works fully integrated with his position at the Foreign Ministry, and said they "must be seen in their entirety, and as a sort of an *uninterrupted chronicle of present times*."[56] The social commitment in these plays, as a "chronicle" of the events, personalities, and conflicts of the first half of the twentieth century, is obvious. It is the substructure and the motivation for Giraudoux's most well-known set of plays, the plays which more than any others have permitted historians to call the period in which they appeared "the Age of Giraudoux."[57]

[56] G. Charensol, "Comment écrivez-vous?" Emphasis added.

[57] Jacques Guicharnaud, *Modern French Theatre*, p. 19. "His plays dominated the French stage all during the thirties and early forties, a time which might be called the Age of Giraudoux."

Four

STYLE

The struggles between destiny and humanity are played out on three distinguishable battlefields: sexual, metaphysical, and political, and each has a characteristic terrain. The sexual plays are by far the most rugged; the opposition is point-blank, and there are no escape routes. The sexual plays are like trench warfare and there is only one trench. The metaphysical terrain is a vertical expansion of the sexual one, and the vertical dimension is infinite. The political terrain is a lateral expansion, which, if not infinite, extends as far as the eye can see. The success of Giraudoux's theater is in large part a measure of the breadth of his palette. The metaphysical and political plays, performed against a panorama of rebounding ideas and glittering theatricality, are more successful than the narrow, sexual dramas. They are also better. This leads to some conclusions.

"Success" has a specific meaning regarding the plays of Giraudoux, a meaning which goes beyond mere commercial advantage. Jouvet says, simply, "There are not *problems* in the theater, there is only one *problem*: success. There is no theater without success."[1] This is not materialistic. To Jouvet and Giraudoux, theater was fundamentally a communication, not a self-expression, and success meant participating communicants. The nature of communication, moreover, puts an emphasis on the medium; and Giraudoux's theater is a theater which resolutely creates and projects a medium, not a philosophy. Giraudoux's celebrated style, in other words, is not simply a vehicle for the transmission of ideas; it is his final product. In his own time this was looked upon as a violation of the fundamental principles of dramaturgy. Now it appears that this was not a violation but a revolution. Giraudoux has survived, the "fundamental principles" have not.

---

[1] Louis Jouvet, *Réflexions du Comédien*, p. 19.

Giraudoux was far more than a littérateur turned playwright. He was a brilliant and important dramatist. He is historic in the theater for two dissimilar reasons; first, as the capstone of the "art theater" movement which had been forty years in search of a playwright, second, as the vital originator of existential drama on dialectical lines—the theater of the absurd, and the theater of cruelty. Like the druggist in his *Intermezzo*, Giraudoux was the man "by whose sole presence the past shakes hands with the most unexpected present" (I:7). Giraudoux culminated one revolution and began the next, and his effect on contemporary concepts of dramatic structure and style, and the relationship between them, has been enormous.

1. Copeau, Jouvet, and the French Theater Renovation

Giraudoux culminated the movement in France to find an artistic, non-naturalistic theater that combined intellectual integrity with poetry, elegance, and visual beauty. In finding a sympathetic producer in Louis Jouvet, Giraudoux was not merely marrying his talent to that of a great director; he was connecting his work with the mainstream of a continuous series of developments toward a new theater aesthetic, whose roots are to be found in discoveries made in the 1880's and 90's.

What is now considered to be the contemporary French theater evolved out of some discoveries by the famous Parisian gas company employee, André Antoine, and, more importantly, out of the reactions against Antoine's discoveries. Antoine started his *Théâtre Libre* in 1887 with the idea of freeing the theater of his day from the hidebound restrictions of commercialism and the well-made play. In so doing, he founded naturalism. This was perhaps not his intention,[2] yet naturalism became entrenched in French theater for the next quarter-century, and Antoine was its *patron*. The counterrevolution was not long in coming, however, and Antoine's supremacy was quickly challenged by an antinaturalistic "art theater" movement, which finally succeeded in displacing him. The first important antinaturalist was the poet Paul Fort, whose *Théâtre d'Art*, formed in 1890, presented "plays" by or adapted from Mallarmé, Shelley, Maeterlinck, Marlowe, and Edgar Allan Poe; performed in front of "scenery" designed by Vuillard,

---

[2] See Antoine, *Mes Souvenirs sur le Théâtre Libre* (Paris: A. Fay et cie., 1921). The *Théâtre Libre* produced all sorts of plays, including comedies, verse melodramas, and a "Punch and Judy" opera. Antoine himself rejected a narrow formula and was mainly interested in producing new plays of many styles. But the reputation of naturalism was indelible.

Bonnard, and Odilon Redon. French theater of the turn of the century wobbled between these two divergent styles, Antoine continuing his work in naturalism, and Fort's antinaturalism, or aestheticism, continued by Lugné Poé at his *Théâtre de l'Œuvre*.

The winning phase of the aesthetic "art" counterrevolution was begun by two literary men, Jacques Rouché and Jacques Copeau, and Jouvet had been deeply involved with both of them. Rouché (who also happened to publish some of the first stories of Giraudoux) wrote extensively about the theatrical renovation occurring in Europe under the direction of men such as Craig, Reinhardt, and Meyerhold, applauding their "beautiful simplifications of decor . . . the stylization, the form, the rhythm, which come together in scenic beauty."[3] He began his *Théâtre des Arts* in 1910 to dignify and simplify the modern French stage with the discoveries he had written about in his reports from abroad. Among the members of his first company were Copeau and Jouvet (and also the actor Charles Dullin), and the company reached an early pinnacle with its production of *The Brothers Karamazov* in Copeau's lasting version. It was Copeau who made the theatrical renovation finally succeed, and the limited success of the *Théâtre des Arts* was superseded by the extraordinary success of Copeau's *Théâtre du Vieux-Colombier*, which opened in Paris in 1913, with Copeau at the helm and Jouvet second in command.

Copeau was a religious mystic who scorned the existing theater for its immorality and ugliness, and created an aesthetic which called for a bare platform and a clear, musical rendition of the text. "The greatest art is . . . to evoke the multiplicity and mystery of life, to draw from things and beings their deeply imbedded song,"[4] he declared, somewhat cryptically, explaining, "it is the essence of drama . . . to be simultaneously word and song, poetry and action, color and dance. To express it by one word, we do as the Greeks and say: Music."[5] Copeau engaged his company six months before their scheduled opening and treated them to a rigorous summer program of training, gymnastics, seminars, and games. He created an ensemble based on one prime maxim: "le texte seul compte,"[6] and he created an architectural stage to do away with the trappings of scenery. Despite his proclivity for the abstract, he was a successful producer, and the *Théâtre du Vieux*

[3] Rouché, *L'Art théâtral moderne* (Paris: E. Cornélie et cie., 1910), p. 4.

[4] Copeau, *Critiques d'un autre temps* (Paris: Nouvelle Revue Française, 1923), p. 230.

[5] France Anders, *Jacques Copeau et le Cartel des Quatre* (Paris, 1959), p. 68.

[6] *Ibid.*, p. 64.

Colombier was immediately acknowledged as the foremost artistic theater in Paris, a reputation it maintained for many years.

The influence of Copeau on the future of French theater was enormously far-reaching:

He completely reformed the acting of actors, the style of directing, and even the conception of the playwright's function. . . . The idea he restored was that theater is fundamentally, above everything else, a *rhythm*, or surrhythm.

The reduction of the decor to hangings and a platform was . . . not so much a stripping down as an emphasis of the "mystique of the gesture." The rediscovery of this metaphysical character of stage production, this theatricality, killed naturalism, and even to an extent realism, in France.[7]

Jouvet was the direct heir to the Copeau tradition, and when Copeau retired in 1924 he passed on the tangible assets of the *Théâtre du Vieux Colombier* to his former assistant, saying in a public testament: "It isn't only a repertory, some collaborators, certain methods of working, a certain artistic viewpoint that I want to give you; it is mainly that *living spirit*, which makes everything inspired by it valuable and beautiful, a spirit without which nothing great can ever be created to last."[8] The living spirit assured the continuity of Rouche—Copeau—Jouvet, and its bearing on the theater of Giraudoux and his successors cannot be overemphasized.

Jouvet took from Copeau the insistence on poetry, music, and pure aestheticism in the theater, and he also shared his former master's concern for the supreme importance of a poetic text, perfectly rendered. He was a serious analyst of dramatic form. His ideas, although in part derivative of Copeau, are unique and explicit, and while they were particularly pertinent to the plays of Giraudoux, they had considerable meaning for the continuation of French drama that followed.

Jouvet writes of the theater as a *fidèle entretien*,[9] implying a communication among the faithful. It is a "passionate contract . . . a communion, a joint participation, a reciprocal interpenetration."[10] His theater is a forum for the interaction of author and audience, actor and spectator; a mutual communion of spirits where harmonies must be established between the life of the drama and the lives of the responders. His direction was guided by aesthetic considerations which were perfectly suited to the Giraudoux style:

[7] Marc Beigbeder, *Le Théâtre en France depuis la Libération*, pp. 37–38.

[8] Anders, *Jacques Copeau*, p. 54.

[9] Jouvet, *Témoignages sur le théâtre*, p. 19.

[10] *Ibid.*, p. 18, 95.

The best direction will permit each spectator to speak his thoughts at leisure, to reenact the play's action later on, and it will give each spectator the freedom to glut himself with feelings and ideas which, consciously or unconsciously, he already possesses.[11]

Jouvet's eminently successful production of Jules Romains' *Knock* (more than one thousand performances) established him as a commercial success and gave him the freedom to support a company, the *Théâtre de l'Athénée*, and to produce a great number of important premieres, including, in addition to most of the plays of Giraudoux, Sartre's *The Devil and the Good Lord*, Cocteau's *The Infernal Machine*, and Genêt's *The Maids*. Yet at the time of his great success with *Knock*, the ironic fact was that the theatrical renovation had been won without a consequent revolution in the writing of plays.

Rouché's, Copeau's and even Paul Fort's companies had languished and died simply because, though they were dedicated to producing new theater, no new drama had come to fill them. While there had been isolated examples of plays dedicated to artistic rather than photographic representation—for example, Jarry's *Ubu* cycle and Cocteau's haphazard forays into the dramatic form—there had been no real gratification of the new school, no aesthetic alliance between the renovated director and a like-thinking author.[12] This is where Giraudoux came in.

Giraudoux was a true participant in this theatrical overhaul, not merely a gentleman diplomat who sent his plays to the theater to be performed. He and Jouvet were allied like soldiers in combat. He wrote plays which were spiritually profound, intellectually honest, and stylistically elegant. Jouvet produced them with a devout attention to the rhythms, gestures, and intonations which would create an aesthetic harmony. They were both rabidly antinaturalistic, dedicated to the

[11] *Ibid.*, p. 69.

[12] The sad case of Paul Claudel must be cited here. Claudel, poet and diplomat, wrote just the sort of plays Copeau was looking for, filled with mystic themes elaborated with Oriental devices, masks, dances, song, and Kabuki variations. But Claudel did not find a sympathetic producer or an audience until many years beyond his time. His early productions under the hands of Lugné-Poé (*L'Annonce faite à Marie* in 1912, *L'Otage* in 1914) and Copeau himself (*L'Échange* in 1914) were failures, and Barrett H. Clark, writing in 1915, failed to list him among the thirteen "well established dramatists" then writing in France (*Modern French Dramatists*, Cincinnati: Stewart and Kidd, 1915, p. x–xi). Only when Jean-Louis Barrault rediscovered Claudel during the Second World War did Claudel come to public and critical attention. Barrault's 1943 production of *Soulier de Satin* at the Comédie Française was a sensation. "What a pity we did not meet forty years earlier," Claudel told Barrault (Barrault, *The Theatre of Jean Louis Barrault*, tr. Joseph Chiari [London: Barrie and Rockliff, 1961], p. 169).

propositions of Copeau in forming an "art" theater, or a "theatrical" theater. Giraudoux, for his part, attended rehearsals assiduously, breathing along with the actors word by word, considering himself "the first of the actors."[13] He collaborated with Jouvet on the germinating ideas of his manuscripts, and on the manuscripts themselves. Jouvet's influence was more indirect than immediate, but by osmosis and indirection the two men worked together to "purify" the theater from naturalism. A co-worker has written:

The alliance between Giraudoux and Jouvet will shine for ages in our memories as one of the rare examples of a recaptured unity. From play to play we have seen the verbal imagination of the one take hold of the scenic imagination of the other. And as a certain Jouvet tone has slipped into Giraudoux's writing, the luminous metaphors of Giraudoux have been translated into Jouvet's designs and directing. He got the impression from Giraudoux that language had regained its original function and could again dispel the shadows. And what Giraudoux had given to language in the way of clarity and certainty, Jouvet returned in exacting interpretation and dazzling illumination.[14]

It was elegant, intellectual, honest, and poetic; far from the meanness of naturalism. Giraudoux's theater is, in fact, a parody of naturalism, with isolated, accidental details accounting for fundamental cosmic forces. Human anguish is described in *Intermezzo* as "collar buttons in revolt," or "saucepans and cleaning fluid," and the awesome series of Argive murders was motivated in *Electra* by Agammemnon's wiry beard and the way he held his pinkie in the air. This was called audacious preciosity, and Giraudoux was frequently criticized for it. But underlying the apparent preciosity is Giraudoux's most important achievement, a reversal of the moralistic naturalist tradition which had stifled dramatic development for at least three hundred years. Giraudoux's revolution on the dramatic front was even greater than Copeau's on the theatrical, and its effect on the following generations of playwrights has been profound.

2. *Giraudoux and the Dramatic Revolution: The Reason for Style*

Marc Beigbeder has said of Copeau, "Instead of making the theatrical gesture cover the daily gesture, as had been the rule, he turned everything topsy-turvy by proclaiming, under the guise of theatricality,

---

[13] Giraudoux, "L'auteur au théâtre," *Littérature*, p. 243.
[14] Georges Neveux, "Le Dialogue Jouvet-Giraudoux," p. 4.

specificity."[15] This is analogous to what Giraudoux did with the writing of plays. The "problem play" was the unwanted inheritance from the realists: a form of theater which communicated ideas on a unilateral basis. This is not inconsistent with the *utile dulce* function of drama explained by Horace, or the body of dramatic theory which grew out of the Renaissance and had ruled the writing of plays since the middle of the seventeenth century with an iron hand. Drama was an instrument for education and moral edification; theatrical characteristics (including the plot) were the mere vehicle for transmission of morals and ideas. Scratch the Scribean sugar coating of a problem play, and you would find a Shavian pill. The *idea* is the end result of this drama, and the plot, characters, and *mise-en-scène* are the means to that end. Copeau and Jouvet attacked this point of view on the theatrical front, and Giraudoux on the dramatic. Giraudoux claimed that *the theatricality itself was the end result*, and that the ideas in a script, no matter how profound or correct, were simply arbitrary structuring devices. This was virtually a Copernican concept, and Giraudoux was widely considered a literary libertine. Claudel, a highly moral dramatist, called Giraudoux "un misérable" for his portrayal of *Judith*, and tried to prevent it from being shown in the same theater that housed his *L'Annonce faite à Marie*. He also wrote a long poem "to avenge the pure and sublime figure of Judith."[16] Claudel, and many others, were interpreting Giraudoux according to traditional systems; they were of the opinion that *Judith* was about Judith. It is not; it is an iconograph of the human condition. The ideas, since they are incapable of resolution, are in a sense arbitrary. What is communicated is some sort of sympathetic vibration between author and audience. What is created for this, and what Giraudoux is properly famous for, is a style.

"People are now looking for a language instead of ideas," he said, adding, "Ideas are already overabundant."[17] The purpose of this language is to appease the *déchirement*, the individual struggle. Giraudoux spoke of this frequently:

People of our day no longer demand of their men of letters mere "works"—the street and the courtyard are full of this sort of abandoned furniture—what they want above all is a language. They no longer wait for the writer, as a fool to a happy king, to tell them "truths." In novels or in pleasant, successful plays

[15] *Le Théâtre en France depuis la Libération*, p. 37.

[16] Claude Roy, "Giraudoux et Dieu," *Cahiers de la Campagnie*, no. 36 (1961), p. 27.

[17] G. Charensol, "Comment écrivez-vous?" *Les Nouvelles Littéraires*, December 11, 1931, p. 12.

... they wait for him to tell them their own truth, to give them a vehicle which will permit them to organize their own thoughts and feelings, to give them his unique secret: style.[18]

This being the case, style, which had heretofore been considered merely an outward form, became the nucleus of the drama; "ideas," heretofore extolled as the rationale for the entire affair, became the framework. Their rightness or wrongness became unimportant. There was to be no moral, no solution, no directive to action. This rationale for drama had been given before, no doubt, but this is the first time it was resolutely announced, defended, and successfully acted upon by a serious dramatist. It is an aesthetic and amoral concept, anathema to dramatic theory since its beginnings: that a play is not a vehicle to promote ideas, but that ideas are the motive power to project a play.[19]

The structural form of Giraudoux's plays is dialectical as opposed to mimetic. The distinction is this: that while mimetic drama takes its cue from Aristotle, and mimes or imitates an action, dialectical drama freezes the action between two equivalent poles. *Oedipus Tyrannos*, which is mimetic, is about an action: Oedipus, in search of his identity, finds it, acts upon it. There is a progression in the text, a general feeling of determined resolution in the ending, and a single-line structure. Dialectical drama contrasts with this. It is nonactive, ambiguous in its conclusions, and complex in its structure. Conclusions, when they come, are arbitrary, and the principal feeling is one of futility and frustration. Thus, in Giraudoux's work, Siegfried is frozen between France and Germany, Judith between sainthood and whoredom, Argos between *justice intégrale* and *justice humaine*, and Hans between the court and the fishes. The staged conclusions to these conflicts are all somewhat arbitrary. The evenness, the joint "rightness" of the opposing

---

[18] "Discours sur le théâtre," *Littérature*, p. 239.

[19] The position of George Bernard Shaw on this subject is of some interest, first because of his historical importance in twentieth-century drama, second because of his self-declared role as an author of a "theater of ideas." Despite the fact that, as with most subjects, Shaw from time to time took both sides of this argument, he has one statement on the relevance of ideas to dramatic art which should be a classic. "Disprove (an) assertion after it is made, yet its style remains. Darwin has no more destroyed the style of Job nor of Handel than Martin Luther destroyed the style of Giotto. All the assertions get disproved sooner or later; and so we find the world full of a magnificent debris of artistic fossils, with the matter-of-fact credibility gone clean out of them, but the form still splendid" (Preface to *Man and Superman*). The present success of Shaw's plays on the stage is a testament to the form of these works, which are certainly fossils as pieces of propaganda, and Shaw's talents were much more devoted to the writing of plays, in his later life, than to the examination of ideas in the abstract. Giraudoux's drama owes a debt to Shaw that has never been properly calculated.

worlds is always emphasized in the dialectical form. It is certainly debatable where dialectical drama got its start, but we remember that the court divided fifty-fifty on Orestes' guilt in Aeschylus' *Orestia*, and the final verdict was given ex machina. Certainly dialectical drama is as old as this, and has coexisted with its mimetic sister throughout the ages.

Mimetic drama relies on its epic sweep or daemonic power in re-creating the great actions which support it. Dialectical drama, not being concerned with great actions, is successful insofar as the playwright suffuses it with vibrant situations and an interesting aroma. "Classical tragedy needs a poetic power that I don't have, and an epic inspiration that I cannot attain," Giraudoux modestly told an interviewer regarding his version of the Greek *Electra*,[20] and he freely admitted that the force of the original was not a part of his structural design. On the contrary, Giraudoux chose to examine the tight, enervating dialectic which prevented his characters from being super-humanly enlarged, and forced him to steer with equanimity and calm between two equally valid courses. His drama is particularly dispassionate and brittle, and relies for its success on the brilliant and beautiful aroma it creates.

The dialectic is a form which theatricalizes naturally. In the drama, unlike narrative, didactic forms, the author can create opposing forces, embody and rationalize them fully, and then let them beat each other's brains out, allowing the audience to draw whatever moral conclusions they wish. In this sense the dialectical drama is like a law trial (and how many plays are simply written from actual trials or in that form) and the audience is the judge and jury. Giraudoux's success in the theater, compared to his relative lack of it in the narrative, is best explained as the easy alliance of his mind with the medium. "The novel does not go well with reasoning or the dialectic," he claimed. "It is a general statement."[21]

It is easy to put these ideas together—Giraudoux's use of dialectical structure and the aestheticism of Copeau and Jouvet. Dialectical drama precludes "philosophizing" and propagandizing; it prevents the uni-lateral transmission of ideas since it discounts the correctness of any single idea. It recognizes that the members of the audience are themselves, emotionally and intellectually, the results of various internal

[20] André Warnod, "J'ai épousseté le buste d'Electre, nous dit M. Jean Giraudoux."
[21] Yvone Moustiers, "Dans les couloirs d'un théâtre, Jean Giraudoux nous parle du roman," p. 2.

compromises between irreconcilable desires, and it reaches an audience not by explanation but by a subtle arousal. Giraudoux's theater is not overwhelming so much as it is undermining. It does not sweep the audience along in a torrent of passion or in an extended line of brilliant reasoning, but it tickles and caresses their minds and feelings until they are replaying the dramatic event and its implications in their own minds, in conscious or subconscious harmony with their own struggles. As Jouvet had called for a theater which allowed each spectator "the freedom to glut himself with feelings and ideas which . . . he already possesses," so Giraudoux wrote, ostensibly about Racine, "The best theater is the one which convinces minds already convinced, which moves already unsettled souls, and which in the end leaves its spectators with the impression of a proof: the proof of their own sensibility and of the age in which they live."[22] Giraudoux's drama, like Jouvet's theater, is addressed not to the masses at large but only to the faithful. It is highly controlled, ritualized according to a set of precepts, and more aesthetic than intellectual.

In this, Giraudoux's drama is churchlike. He sought in the theater a lay religion in which the metaphysical struggles of human life could be played out in a theatrical ceremony. It is at this level that Giraudoux most closely corresponds to the mystical Copeau (who left the theater answering a call to a more conventional religion)[23] and where his drama can be seen as more than a collection of witty metaphors and apothegms. His drama is a religious communication among believers, and not an attempt to convert the heathen or recalcitrant drama critics. As it involves believers, it involves a common experience, a familiar set of rules, given texts and ritualized reenactment. The common experience is not the fall from Eden (Giraudoux is creating a *lay* religion) but the loss of innocence and the unapproachable nature of destiny. Writes Giraudoux, "the theater is like a Catholic Mass of language. No more than the Mass does it need minute scrutiny for comprehension. The only thing it must not do is let the faith grow cold."[24] The dialectic leads to celebration, not understanding; it is

[22] "Racine," *Littérature*, p. 38.

[23] "I left the theater as I had left my family when I was twenty. And as a loving husband leaves his wife, in order to answer a call stronger than love. I didn't even know then what the call was," says Copeau in *Souvenirs du Vieux-Colombier* (Paris, Nouvelles éditions latines 1931), p. 104. Copeau left in part in disgust at the mechanics of a commercial enterprise, in part because of Jouvet's withdrawal from the company, but mainly to satisfy a religious conversion and the "call" attendant upon it.

[24] André Rousseaux, "Entre le théâtre et le roman avec M. Jean Giraudoux."

bilateral; it warms the faith of the faithful in an organized, ritualistic way.

The function of religion that Giraudoux invokes is an aesthetic one. This is a function rarely promulgated by defenders of the faith, yet it is central to European Catholicism to be the patron and repository of the greatest examples of Western creativity. The function of the cathedral in Europe is highly aesthetic. The cathedrals of both Paris and Bellac provide the same respite from the chaotic commercial world: a gathering of horizontal and vertical space wherein all is harmonic, peaceful, and beautiful; infused with ghostly silence to ease the torments of a fractured world. Architecture, appointment, and the *mise en scène* of the cathedral experience provide this soothing to the *déchirements* of the workaday world to believer and nonbeliever alike; the rightness or wrongness of the dogma is a negligible issue in the cool and stilly silence of *Notre Dame* or *St. Etienne's*.

Giraudoux's drama is comparable to the aesthetic function of the Church in two ways. First it is a respite from reality, a world apart from the grueling conditions of daily life. Second, it is based solidly in the human condition. The celebration of the dialectic, like the celebration of the mass, does not ignore man's plight in the universe. The European cathedral has its meaning in the crucifix, which is always present above the altar. The building itself is in the form of a crucifix, reminding the faithful at every moment of the supreme moment of human agony, the tearing apart between faith and reason which is represented in the Bible by a single cry, "My God, My God, why hast thou forsaken me?" As the Church celebrates this moment, Giraudoux's theater celebrates the similar tearing apart which comes with the realization of the nature of human existence. The highly aesthetic nature of both media make them invaluable; the recognition of essential human agony keeps them honest, keeps them from being mere cultural playgrounds.

Giraudoux's was a religion stripped of God, with the magic of theatricality in His place. His drama was conceived on the same framework as conventional religions, but it took nontheistic proportions.

The theater is the . . . only means by which the humblest and most illiterate public can be put in personal contact with the highest conflicts, and to create for itself a lay religion with a liturgy and saints.[25]

---

[25] "Discours sur le théâtre," *Littérature*, p. 233.

Do not be mistaken. The rapport between the theater and religious solemnizing is obvious; it was not by chance that our first plays were performed on the steps of our cathedrals. You could find no better place for them.[26]

The religious model established Giraudoux's theater as a place of communion, not instruction. Instruction is left to Sunday schools; the Mass celebrates. Giraudoux, following this concept, could in fact limit himself to the "highest conflicts," and focus on metaphysical themes, which need nothing in the way of logical explanation (since none could be effective), but profit from ritualization as the Greeks and medieval poets had done.

Giraudoux's themes are the eternal ones. Although *Siegfried* is undeniably about political issues, and *Sodom and Gomorrah* about marital ones, both plays are most deeply involved with the universal conflicts involved when ideologies clash with realities. Giraudoux was rarely as interested in his characters as people as he was in their participation in the eternal conflict. "There are no great men, there are only great conflicts," he once said,[27] and the universal, tragic conflict between the promise of youth and the disappointment of age was his main working ground. This took a number of forms: France versus Germany, war versus peace, sex versus marriage, sex versus no sex; yet in each case the theme is profoundly tied to the unknown and the metaphysical. Jouvet described this sort of drama as "a playing with the reflections of the human and a refraction of the universal."[28] Jouvet, who was also admired for his productions of *Tartuffe* and *School for Wives*, wrote, relative to the themes of those plays and of Giraudoux's:

All the grand themes are spiritual, and I never believe in a play, nor a *mise-en-scène*, which is not conceived with a little more than our everyday sounds, a little more than our everyday sights. The passion of Athalie, of Phèdre, or the sentiments of Alceste and Tartuffe are always valid and fecund because they are obscure, as are all the heroes of the theater, and as we are ourselves.[29]

"Grand themes" were what Giraudoux worked with and he needed a "grand style" to support them.

3. The Giraudoux Style: Outward Forms

The style of Giraudoux's drama reflects its dialectical structure, its aestheticism, its stated emphasis on form, its neoreligious purpose, and

[26] "Visitations," *Œuvres littéraires diverses*, p. 710.
[27] "Les Cinq tentations de La Fontaine," *Œuvres littéraires diverses*, p. 324.
[28] *Témoignages sur le théâtre*, p. 84.
[29] *Ibid.*, pp. 85–86.

its universal themes. As an entity in itself, it is well known; Giraudoux, like Shaw, has been both praised and damned as essentially a stylist. He himself gloried in it. "Without style nothing lives, and nothing survives: everything is in *le style*," he claimed.[30] This follows. Since Giraudoux proclaimed it was a language, not a set of ideas which he wanted to bequeath, it is not the metaphysics, but the theatricalization of the metaphysics in which we are interested. This was the Giralducien style. Six of its elements may be profitably distinguished: beauty, literariness, theatricalism, subjectivity, magic/fantasy, and language.

Giraudoux's plays were beautiful in a quite specific sense. They were *meant* to be beautiful. Jouvet, who shared none of Copeau's scenic Jansenism, collaborated with the most luxurious designers in Paris for the Giraudoux premieres. *Ondine*, which was designed by Pavel Tchelitchev and had music by Henri Sauget, was one of the most lavish productions Paris had seen, and Claude Bérard's celebrated designs for *The Madwoman*, supplemented by a citywide appeal for costumes and properties, led to the first "spectacular" of the postwar stage. Without question, Giraudoux's plays were the most handsomely dressed and mounted productions seen in Paris between the wars and through the early forties, and this was a not insignificant factor in their commercial success. Yet beauty is a fundamental element of Giraudoux's dramaturgy, it is not merely a commercial appendage. The tragedy of Hans, for example, is that Ondine is utterly beautiful. If this is not true, the play ceases to exist. Not only is Ondine herself beautiful, but also her house in the forest is beautiful and the song of the lesser Ondines is beautiful. The poem of the kitchen girl is beautiful. Since Giraudoux is describing the tragic course of a man who leaves a beautiful world of destiny only to found an ugly one of humanity, he must create that beauty aurally and visually if he is to do more than indicate a philosophical position. He must create beauty in order to dramatize it.

Not the least beautiful aspect of Giraudoux's works is the literary polish of the writing, the "literariness" of the plays. For this too he has been damned as well as praised, for literary preciosity has been the downfall of many men of letters who have attempted to write for the stage. With Giraudoux it becomes more help than harm. The literary devices are multifold, varying from the incredibly elaborate *tirade* to the simple use of repetition and opposition, for example:

[30] Paul Morand, *Adieu à Giraudoux*, p. 15.

Hans: Vous, la dignité! Vous, l'orgueil!
Bertha: Moi, l'humilité! Moi, l'impudence! [*Ondine*, II:4]

or simple verse, for example:

First little girl: Depuis dix-neuf ans elle amasse Dans sa bouche un crachat
fielleux.
Second little girl: Elle pense à tes limaces, Jardinier, pour saliver mieux.
[*Electra*, I:1]

In fact the individual devices—metaphor, rhyme, aphorism, pathetic
fallacy, and their fellows—are not important so much as a general
literary tone which assures the audience that every line is not merely
uttered, it is turned. Giraudoux's revival of the dramatic *tirade* was a
signal achievement. The Giralducien *tirade* may be defined as a long set
speech with two characteristics: the elusiveness of the subject and the
dogged precision of its explanation. This literary showmanship takes
imagination, impudence, and irreverent wit in quantities rarely col-
lected in the contemporary theater. But the *tirade* is within the basic
rhythm of the play and virtually all of the speeches in Giraudoux are
little *tirades*. His language leaves no impression of recaptured conversation. Two short speeches from *Intermezzo* may be used to illustrate this—one represents the point of view of humanity, the other of
destiny; neither represents a speech coming from a human being in the
observable world.

Inspector: Spirits, form of space and eggwhites (you see, I don't mince my
words—if they have any dignity at all they will know what they're
supposed to do) humanity in my person defies you to appear! You are
going to be given a unique occasion, if you lend us your presence, to
regain a little credit in the arrondissement. I am not going to ask you
to take a living parrot from my pocket—the classical operation of
spirits, it seems. I just want you to make a sparrow fly from this tree,
from this forest, when I count three. I am counting: one ... two ...
three. You see, it's lamentable! (*His hat flies off*) God, what a wind!
[I:4]
Isabelle: Among those who have passed on about me, there are some who
I sensed right away would be gone forever, stricken from the list of
the living and the dead. I have sent them into oblivion like stones. But
there are others whom I have sent into death as on a mission, a challenge,
whose deaths seemed to me, on the contrary, a road to understanding.
The atmosphere of a voyage, and of an unknown continent, floated
around their graves. I could not say goodbye to them with words,

only with gestures. All afternoon, I found myself occupied with them
as they discovered new climates, new flora. It was sunny, and all of a
sudden I saw them being warmed, in their world, by their new sun.
It rained, and they received the first drops of an infernal rain. [II:6]

Giraudoux uses language as a pure, plastic medium and he shapes it to
his purposes quite irrespective of its naturalistic functions. From a
naturalistic point of view, both preceding speeches are preposterous,
not only because of their subject matter, but also their mode of expression. Even "realistic" scenes share this literary elaboration:

Zelten: Voila!
Robineau: Voila!
Zelten: Is that you? Robineau, Hippolyte-Amable?
Robineau: Otto-Wilhelmus von Zelten-Buchenbach, it's me.
Zelten: Is it you, brown brachycephalus, overloaded with eye-glasses and
    wool waistcoats, terrible in the attack?
Robineau: Yes, cream of culture, butter of carnage, son of Arminius, it is I.
    [*Siegfried*, I:6]

This writing is perhaps not unexpected for an accomplished man of
letters; what *is* unexpected is that it works successfully in the theater.
This was the universal shock of *Siegfried*, that literary elegance, even
preciosity, could be integrated into serious drama without harm, in
fact, with revolutionary success. Obviously, this was a reversal of the
naturalistic concept, and one of the first persons to realize *Siegfried*'s
importance was André Antoine himself. Writing in the journal
Information shortly after the opening, Antoine remarked, "The arrival
of M. Jean Giraudoux in the theater is an event which will have profound repercussions on the present dramatic movement; I find the
same sort of revolutionary impression that was caused by François de
Curel's bursting forth with realism in 1891."[31] Giraudoux's revolution
was not merely bringing literacy to the stage but, in creating a literary
language that could express more than naturalistic conversation, it was
an attempt to use words for their symbolic, rather than representational
value. Giraudoux called his language a language of signs not words,
the sign incorporating into itself more than verbal powers:

We must be aware of the importance of the sign in literary language.
There is a great difference between literary language, which is composed of
signs, and ordinary language, which is composed of indications. Indications are

---

[31] Robert de Beauplan, "*Siegfried* à la Comédie des Champs-Elysées."

analytic and tend to lose themselves in confusion and approximation. The sign is synthetic; it gathers in itself the sense of whatever it means, and makes this perceptible by some sort of commotion. The language of the sign is somewhat magical, something of the sorcerer's language, and that is why the sign predominates in the theater. The public, sitting before the closed curtain, is not waiting for explanations. It is waiting for a sign by which everything will be made clear. . . .

Jouvet and I have worked together for several years. All our efforts with our company have been to give the language of the theater this force of signs, which establishes the contact with the public. We ask our actors not to be speakers, but magicians.[32]

The sign was his contribution; by it he meant not only words, but whole *tirades* themselves. It was a shaping of the medium (language) to express content by commotion rather than explication. Theatricalism was simply a broader, more inclusive, means of creating that commotion.

Theatricalism has a special meaning (as distinguished, that is, from theatricality). It refers to the use of the theater, and theatrical conventions, as more than neutral media; and it refers to that whole list of self-conscious theatrical allusions which serve to remind the spectator that he is in a theater watching a play—not peeping in on a domestic quarrel. The gardener in *Electra* comes out between acts to say:

> I'm not in the play anymore. That's why I'm free to come and tell
> you what the play isn't able to tell you. [*Electra, Entr'acte*]

He goes on to discuss the nature of tragedy, and the nature of *Electra*. It is a novel device (although certainly not without precedent) and it demonstrates in an unambiguous way that the playwright is happy to let the audience be continuously aware of the medium in which he is working. The same effect can be seen when the chamberlain in *Ondine* calls for an intermission and the curtain falls on Act Two, or when the curtain falls half way and then rises in *The Trojan War*. The play-within-the-play, another device to keep us aware of where we are, is used extensively in *Ondine* and *Electra*; the "production number" is included and somehow justified in *Intermezzo* (the "Fugue for the Provincial Chorus," the "Song of the Dandified Hangmen"), in *Judith* (the deification ceremony), in *The Madwoman of Chaillot* (the trial scene ending in *La Belle Polonaise*), and indeed in most of the other

---

[32] Rousseaux, "Entre le théâtre et le roman."

plays. Giraudoux does not merely stand at the edge of the proscenium, he steps out and turns on the houselights. He continually refers to other plays: *Faust, The School for Wives, Medea, Phèdre,* and *Athalie,* and he frequently refers to other plays of his own as well. He associates himself with theatrical traditions; indeed, many of his plays are adaptations of classical works, and he emphasizes that they are so, to wit: *Amphitryon 38.*

Theatricalism was nothing new in France at this time—Cocteau, Claudel, Jarry, and Vitrac were all experimenting with various theatricalist ideas. Giraudoux's uniqueness was his ability to integrate it with other stylistic elements in the creation of a viable aesthetic. Theatricalism as a simple technique is of faddish importance and often is quickly forgotten. There are exceptions, however, and they are important ones. Pirandello successfully used theatricalist techniques to exploit the confusion between internally and externally perceived "reality," and Brecht, some years later, forged theatricalist drama to maintain audience focus on current political situations. Giraudoux shared these motives, but had an overriding one besides. It was a theater itself that he wanted to project, a theater which was a medium for the temporary calming of dialectic-shattered nerves. Theatricalism proclaims the theater as a useful tool. "There are those who dream, but for those who don't, there is the theater,"[33] he claimed once; and it should not be surprising that his theater calls attention to itself in a bold way.

The beauty, literariness, and theatricalism of Giraudoux's theater attempted to reach the audience by nonintellectual means. Despite his enormous mentality, Giraudoux never wrote rational dramas; nor are his plays, as some have claimed, superrational. They are irrational, plain and simple, and calculated to work into the minds and feelings of their spectators by subtle, subjective paths. "The word 'understand' does not exist in the theater," Giraudoux has Jouvet say in *The Paris Impromptu* (Scene 3), which is a play specifically about the art of writing and producing plays, namely Giraudoux's, and this is a sincerely meant dictum. "The true public does not understand, they feel . . . those who want to understand in the theater are those who do not understand the theater" (Scene 3), he continues; and to André Rousseaux he complains about critics, "they want to understand—but it is only necessary to feel."[34] Arguments in Giraudoux are not really arguments, and they

[33] "Discours sur le théâtre," p. 233.
[34] "Entre le théâtre et le roman."

are incapable of intellectual adjudication. The love between Hans and Ondine is neither rational nor rationally defensible: it is simply felt. The passion for justice which Electra feels cannot be successfully argued before impersonal judges, nor can Geneviève's argument to Siegfried nor Hector's to Helen. Indeed, the conflicts which Giraudoux draws are often between an intellectual line of reasoning and an emotional pastiche of feelings; the drama is not one of debate but of moral and emotional reactions.

Giraudoux's plays appeal to the eye and ear as well as to the mind— this is why their physical representation has been deemed so essential to their success. The battering of ideas in his dialectic produces no academic conclusions; it simply sets up rhythms and harmonies, which are then exploited on the stage. Jouvet once claimed that "the goal of the theater cannot be a search for intellectual order, but rather a revelation of an order of the senses."[35] Giraudoux effectively seduces our senses in the savoir faire manner of a polished roué. He lulls, coddles, pricks, tantalizes, dazzles, and withdraws, leaving us with an impression of having been very much moved without having been physically approached. If knowledge is to be transmitted, it is not in the theater, but afterward, after a prolonged filtration through the spectator's subconscious. "You will understand *tomorrow*," says "Jouvet" in the *Impromptu:*

> Sometimes when I'm taking the bus to the theater, I notice a good-looking old gentleman arm in arm with a young girl. Their steps are lively and animated, their radiant faces beam at one another; I am sure that they must have seen a good play the night before. They didn't understand it, perhaps. But because of the play they understand everything today—the beautiful weather, life, the leaves on the trees, the ears on the horses. . . . It was a well-written play, obviously.
> [Scene 3]

The combination of sensual, subjective, and theatricalist impulses preclude "realism" as a style, and Giraudoux made no attempt to work toward naturalistic justification for these "unreal" theatrical elements. He went the other way, into the realm of fantasy and magic. Even in *Siegfried*, the most naturalistic of all his plays, the first critics praised "first of all, the fantasy, which is uninhibited and goes where it wants."[36]

[35] Jouvet, "Pourquoi j'ai monté Tartuffe," *Témoignages sur le théâtre*, p. 85.

[36] Gérard d'Houville in *Le Figaro*, quoted in De Beauplan, "*Siegfried* à la Comédie des Champs-Elysées."

All of Giraudoux's plays include scenes of fantasy—angels and arch-angels in the biblical plays, errant gods and goddesses in the Greek ones, and the spirits of the friends of vegetables in *The Madwoman of Chaillot*. *Ondine* and *Intermezzo* are fantasies created out of whole cloth, purely original fantasies similar to *The Birds* and *The Tempest*.

There is an aspect of Giraudoux's fantasy which is purely romantic. *Ondine*, for example, is at one level a very simple and moving love story. The romantic impulse is in all his works; he describes the other-worldly romance of men with animals (*Ondine*), with justice (*Electra*), with their childhoods (*Siegfried*), and with their universe (*Intermezzo*). His plays cast us back to the ancient worlds of Greece, Troy, Sodom, and Bethulia, and yet fill us with nostalgia for the simple sounds of yesterday. Certainly there was no attempt on his part to reproduce the details of contemporary life. For him a seat at the theater should have "the extraterritoriality of an embassy in the antique or heroic realm, in the domains of the illogical and the fantastic."[37] But the fantasy of Giraudoux is not escapist. It is an attempt to find a reality deeper than words can wield. "The theater, that's being real in the unreal", said little Vera (*Paris Impromptu*, Scene 1), and Giraudoux had no other dramatic intentions. Visions of childhood innocence, passions for un-realizable ideals, longings for unity with the natural kingdom; these are as real as structured political societies, he reasoned, and his drama was a search for a broader, profounder picture of reality than the realists portrayed. The heritage of the *Théâtre Libre* he found contradictory and offensive.

Dasté: That was something, the Free Theater! Someone said it was five
    o'clock, and they had a real clock ring out five o'clock. Some freedom!
Raymone: If the clock rang a-hundred-and-two o'clock, then it would begin
    to be theater. [*The Paris Impromptu*, Scene 1]

This is not the fantasy of Barrie, but of Ionesco. Giraudoux's fantastic vision is never one of fairies and big rock-candy mountains—it is a perverse world of demonic evils that tempt, torture, and destroy a poor human creature. Giraudoux uses magic, but it is black magic. The sweetness of romantic fantasy never is permitted to prevail.

This distinguishes Giraudoux not only from Barrie but from the entire school of sentimental humanism. This has not been widely

---

[37] "Discours sur le théâtre," pp. 239–40.

recognized; Sartre, for example, called Giraudoux a "pagan eudae-monist."[38] While not exactly fighting words, the label is incorrect, and perhaps more applicable to Sartre than to Giraudoux. Giraudoux's venture into the illogical and fantastic universe is not a flight from reality but a plunge into the absurd.

4. Giraudoux, the Absurd, and the Cruel

It has not been customary to think of Giraudoux as an absurdist, a label which is fairly loose of definition, but it is certain that he was probing the absurd condition in as dramatic a way as anyone after him. The "absurd" is a condition of man that has been described to most general satisfaction by Albert Camus in his essay "The Myth of Sisyphus," which has had a large effect on contemporary French drama.[39] Camus writes, "the absurd . . . is that divorce between the mind that desires and the world that disappoints, my nostalgia for unity, this fragmented universe, and the contradiction which binds them together."[40] This is a purely philosophical position, directly parallel with Giradoux's comment, quoted at the beginning of this study, that tragedy is "the affirmation of a horrible bond between humanity and a greater-than-human destiny." Both Camus's "absurd," and Giraudoux's "tragedy" are born of this contradiction and conflict between ideals and action, between desire and accomplishment. The dialectic does not exist either in the world or in man, but in their con-frontation. The absurd is the admission of man's failure to come to an intellectual understanding of existence. It reaffirms subjective self-definition, and discounts rationality. Camus, himself a dramatist of some importance, considered the absurd not only a philosophic truth, but the dramatic structure of human life. "The appetite for the absolute illustrates the essential impulse of the human drama," he wrote.[41] The absurd is a way of looking at things, a way which is eminently theatrical, as Giraudoux was able to prove. His dramaturgy is based on man's appetite for the absolute, and it is unresolved in that the absolute is

[38] "M. Jean Giraudoux et la philosophie d'Aristote." Eudaemonism is a system of ethics which relates moral obligations to happiness.

[39] See Martin Esslin, *The Theatre of the Absurd* (New York: Doubleday, 1961), esp. pp. xix–xx, and William I. Oliver, "Between Absurdity and the Playwright," in T. Bogard and W. I. Oliver, *Modern Drama* (New York: Oxford University Press, 1965).

[40] *The Myth of Sisyphus*, translated by Justin O'Brien (New York: Random House, 1960), p. 37.

[41] *Ibid.*, p. 13.

never achieved, the appetite never satiated. This ambiguity, this failure to conclude a dramatic action, leads directly to the absurd in its original sense of "futile." Fantasy is no escape; it is merely a mechanism for expressing the absolute, the human propulsion. Man carries within him his own fantasies, but his enactment of them is futile, absurdly dramatic. This is the fantasy and "antirealism" of Giraudoux: a fantasy of the absurd, of the impossible, of the madly ringing clocks of Ionesco's *Bald Soprano*—a symbol of the absurd which Giraudoux himself anticipated by ten years.

The depiction of the absurd condition has been the job of the existentialists, Camus among them; the workers in the field have been the absurdist dramatists, Ionesco among them. Camus approached the absurd logically, Ionesco approached it absurdly, being a victim of the same circumstances in which he found his characters. In other words, with the absurd dramatists, both content and form are absurd. Giraudoux's discovery that fantasy could be a viable form for dramatizing a serious human condition was an important weapon in the hands of the absurdists who followed him, and the line from Giraudoux to Anouilh to Ionesco is fairly easy to follow.

From existentialism to absurdity is but a step, and the theater of cruelty just a step beyond that. Existentialism recognizes the absurd and tries to find ways to meet it. Absurdity accepts the absurd and submits to it. Cruelty adopts the absurd and becomes its blood brother. Cruelty uses absurdity as a weapon. The theater of cruelty involves a certain amount of complicity with the absurd, and a willingness to exploit it for dramatic and theatrical purposes. Giraudoux anticipated all of this. In 1953 Ionesco wrote, as part of a tribute to Giraudoux,

In *Ondine* . . . the cruelty—since at this moment everyone is talking about a theater of cruelty—remains intact; never has the theme of separation, of love, of absence, of death (more than death, for there is something even more atrocious, the retroactive suppression of an essential event, torn to atoms, dissolved in the universe, rejected into the nothingness of cosmic oblivion: life, not only extinguished but returned to the increate, never to have been at all), never has this theme appeared to me more unbearable."[42]

The theater of cruelty, which everyone was *not* talking about in Giraudoux's time, has generally been attributed to the Cassandra-like voice of Antonin Artaud, a true madman of the theater, who produced little yet influenced much. Artaud's volume of essays entitled *The Theater and Its Double* blue prints a cryptic theater of cruelty, and has

[42] "J'aime Giraudoux."

been widely influential since his death. Despite a wildly inchoate style, however, his ideas are not dissimilar to Giraudoux's and the points of resemblance are striking. In many ways, Giraudoux was creating the theater of cruelty which Artaud was clamoring for, but without the noisy ostentation that went with it.

Artaud, in a now well known allusion, compares the theater to the plague: "Like the plague it reforges the chain between what is and what is not, between the virtuality of the possible and what already exists in materialized nature."[43] This is both existentialist and Giralducien; whether the theater "reforges a chain" or "affirms a tie" is simply a question of the better metaphor. To both, the theater is the place where "what is" and "what is not" come crashing together.

Artaud realized his "theater of cruelty" was subject to misinterpretation, and he qualified his remarks extensively:

As soon as I have said "cruelty," everyone will at once take it to mean "blood." But "theater of cruelty" means a theater difficult and cruel for myself first of all. And on the level of performance, it is not the cruelty we can exercise upon each other by hacking at each other's bodies . . . but the much more terrible and necessary cruelty which things can exercise against us. We are not free. And the sky can still fall on our heads. And the theater has been created to teach us that first of all.[44]

Artaud's seminal thoughts have not been very much followed, even by his most self-declared ardent devotees. Theater of cruelty has often been an indulgent series of rapings, killings, insane behavior, and a stage doused with more blood than has graced the stage since Middleton, and even Artaud's drama with its torture wheels and exploding vaginas has hardly been "cruel for myself, first of all." Nevertheless, his theater of cruelty, which he admitted had to be begun with "crude means" in order to attract attention,[45] has a religious tone. He called for "a religious idea of the theater . . . capable of recovering within ourselves those energies which ultimately create order and increase the value of life."[46] He proposed, to counter the impossibilities of rational communication, a "total" theater, a "poetry in space," a "poetry of the senses," a "language of gestures and postures, dance and music."[47]

[43] *The Theater and Its Double*, translated by Mary Caroline Richards (New York: Grove Press, 1958), p. 27. (Originally *Le Théâtre et son double*, Paris, 1938. The collection includes essays in the main written in the early 1930's.)

[44] *Ibid.*, p. 79.

[45] *Ibid.*, p. 81.

[46] *Ibid.*, p. 80.

[47] *Ibid.*, pp. 37, 38.

Dispensing with ordinary verbal communication (words, he said, should have "approximately the importance they have in dreams"[48]), Artaud replaces it with the theater of the "sign-language," a "pure theatrical language which does without words, a language of signs, gestures and attitudes having an ideographic value."[49] The objects of this communication are not facts but universal fantasies: "the public will believe in the theater's dreams on condition that it takes them for true dreams and not for a servile copy of reality; on condition that they allow the public to liberate within itself the magical liberties of dreams."[50] The result: "A theater which, abandoning psychology recounts the extraordinary, stages natural conflicts, natural and subtle forces, and presents itself first of all as an exceptional power of re-direction."[51]

Artaud's "manifesto" for a theater of cruelty, despite its intentional virulence, follows closely the more conventional lines of Craig, Copeau, and Jouvet, and the proximity of his ideas to Giraudoux's, while not indicating an influence from one to the other, clarifies the line in which Giraudoux and Jouvet were both working.[52] Although Artaud speaks repeatedly of Oriental models, his theater is entirely Western in its theoretical conception,[53] and the "theater of cruelty" is strictly a European phenomenon.

Giraudoux himself scorned manifestos, and he wrote plays the way he wanted to without much concern with polemics. The self-criticism we find in his work was either snapped up by interviewers over twenty years or was buried in various works of nonfiction and drama. His essays on the theater are only half-serious commentaries and are rarely specific. Yet the actual plays of Giraudoux, together with these works, form an impressive body of dramatic theory and one which is directly

[48] *Ibid.*, p. 94.

[49] *Ibid.*, p. 39.

[50] *Ibid.*, p. 86.

[51] *Ibid.*, p. 83.

[52] The two men are almost never mentioned together, yet they were fairly close contemporaries. Though Giraudoux was sixteen years the elder, their first works in the theater occurred in the late 1920's. The bulk of Artaud's *Theatre and Its Double* was written by 1933; Giraudoux's "Discours sur le théâtre" was delivered in 1931.

[53] Artaud continually brings in examples of Balinese theater, which treats, in his words, "the struggles of a soul preyed upon by ghosts and phantoms from the beyond." This description applies as well to Giraudoux's work. Perhaps the most important source of Artaud's ideas, however, was his experience in silent films. No one who has witnessed his performance in Dreyer's *La Passion de Jeanne d'Arc* and remembers his final posture, holding the crucifix aloft as Joan burns, will fail to understand the communicative power of an ideographic gesture.

related to the major trends of dramatic writing today. It is not important whether Giraudoux was an existentialist, absurdist, or a "cruelist"; such definitions are impossible to stick to any major dramatist without benumbing qualifications. But his contribution in these areas should be recognized. It highlights the line of development from Jarry to Ionesco, a broader line than is generally granted, and it reflects the boldness of Giraudoux's plays as individual and contemporary works. Giraudoux anticipated artistic developments as well as he did political and social ones; his plays can be appreciated now more seriously, perhaps, than they were in his time.

He returned magic and fantasy to the theater in an honest and meaningful way. He discovered the *reason* for fantasy's theatricality: because the human being naturally fantasizes. In so doing, he made fantasy real—more real than naturalism.

He promulgated the absurd ambiguous drama, which was its own excuse for existing and taught no moral. *The Trojan War* is not antiwar; it merely presents the dialectic of war. *Ondine* presents the dialectic of love. Decisions in these cases are arbitrary ones; Giraudoux permitted himself no dishonesty. He saw that truth was not simply one side or the other, but the dialectic itself: that Zeus would not agree with Apollo or Athena, but with both of them and neither of them. He presented this in its entirety.

Giraudoux has often been presented as a dedicated "liberal," a humanist, a gentle sentimentalist. A recent author, for example, writes "*Electra* ends on an ironic note. The Eumenides have shown the sister of Oreste that she has nothing but her justice, but of what use is justice if thousands of innocent people die to attain it? Giraudoux was too much of a humanist to believe that the end justifies the means."[54] But Giraudoux not only believed it, he knew it. His was not a theater of humanism but a theater of cruelty, where the humane man may rue the tragic discord in human lives, but he cannot oppose it, or gloss over it.

He presented life as a cruel and tragic adventure, a continual frustration, which could only be assuaged by suicide. He spared little in this presentation, for, with the exception of *The Madwoman*, none of his plays ends happily. Yet, most importantly, he found that the tragic adventure could be both funny and gay. "Jean Giraudoux is the only man of the twentieth century capable of writing tragedies and having

[54] Robert Emmet Jones, *The Alienated Hero in Modern French Drama*, pp. 86–87.

them applauded,"[55] wrote one highly sympathetic critic, and Giraudoux never wallowed in despair at man's fate, but presented it audaciously and ironically. His is the prototype of the "tragic farce," the "comic tragedy," which has become the standard genre-form of the absurdists of the 50's and 60's. "All the genres are mixed up in the modern drama," said Giraudoux in *Siegfried* (I:8). Sartre and Camus have used the theater to point out possible responses to the absurd; Giraudoux makes the theater itself that response.

He creates, with wit and an elegant sense of beauty, a golden dramaturgy to express and discharge anxiety. Ionesco noted this, I think wisely:

This marvelous beauty which we are thankful that Giraudoux possessed, gave to the unhappiness of human life a pitiless character, a frozen anguish, an exemplary testament. What is more horrible than the knowledge of the complete futility of our despair, of our existence, our not going anywhere, not being registered in any logbook of the universe, of any god? There is no other drama than this. However, if complicity with this sordidness is the acceptance of our shame, beauty is our only honor. I love Giraudoux.[56]

In the end, Giraudoux's importance is neither as the capstone of the theatrical renovation nor as the initiator of the dramatic one, but as a hugely gifted individual dramatist, who saw the world from a unique perspective combining political, moral, and philosophical values, and created a glorious dramaturgy to house them.

[55] Georges-Albert Astre, "Note sur Jean Giraudoux, poète tragique," p. 174.
[56] "J'aime Giraudoux."

Bibliography

A superb bibliography of Giraudoux's published works, plus the major critical studies on that work, has been compiled by René Marill Albérès and Laurent Le Sage, and appears in Albérès' *Ésthetique et morale chez Jean Giraudoux* (Paris: Nizet, 1957), pp. 505–26. This bibliography lists 262 separate publications by Giraudoux, including prepublications and posthumous editions and collections. It also annotates more than a hundred critical studies (rating them as one-star, two-star, or three-star studies according to M. Albérès' preferences) and divides them by categories. Rather than attempt to duplicate this definitive work, I have chosen simply to indicate where Giraudoux's work can be found in English translation or adaptation, and list my own major sources for this study.

Where the reader is able to work with the original French, Giraudoux's plays are now available in two separate complete editions:

Giraudoux, Jean. *Théâtre complet.* 16 vols. Neuchâtel et Paris: Ides et Calendes, 1945–53. This collection includes four volumes of variants.
———. *Théâtre.* 4 vols. Paris: Grasset, 1958–59.

Most of Giraudoux's nondramatic work is available in the following post-humous collections:

Giraudoux, Jean. *Œuvre romanesque.* 2 vols. Paris: Grasset, 1955. Includes all the novels and many stories.
———. *Œuvres littéraires diverses.* Paris: Grasset, 1958. Includes most literary essays, including the earlier collections, *Littérature* and *Visitations.*
———. *De Pleins Pouvoirs à Sans Pouvoirs.* Paris: Gallimard, 1950. Includes the late political essays.

I. PLAYS OF GIRAUDOUX IN ENGLISH TRANSLATION OR ADAPTATION (by date of original publication)

Siegfried (1928)
    (1) translated by Philip Carr. New York: Dial Press, 1930.

(2) translated by Phyllis La Farge and Peter H. Judd, in Jean Giraudoux, *Three Plays*, vol 2. New York: Hill and Wang, 1964.

Amphitryon 38 (1929)
(1) translated by S. N. Behrman. New York: Random House, 1938.
(2) translated by Phyllis La Farge and Peter H. Judd, in Jean Giraudoux, *Three Plays*, vol. 2. New York: Hill and Wang, 1964.
(3) translated by Roger Gellert, in Jean Giraudoux, *Plays*, vol. 2. London: Oxford University Press, 1967.

Judith (1931)
(1) translated by John K. Savacool, in *The Modern Theatre*, ed. Eric Bentley, vol. 3. New York: Anchor, 1955.
(2) translated by Christopher Fry, in *The Drama of Jean Giraudoux*, vol. 1. London: Oxford University Press, 1963.

Intermezzo (1933)
(1) translated by Maurice Valency as *The Enchanted*, in Jean Giraudoux, *Four Plays*, vol. 1. New York: Hill and Wang, 1958.
(2) translated by Roger Gellert, in Jean Giraudoux, *Plays*, vol 2. London: Oxford University Press, 1967.

La Guerre de Troie n'aura pas lieu (1935)
(1) translated by Christopher Fry as *Tiger at the Gates*, in *The Drama of Jean Giraudoux*, vol 1. London: Oxford University Press, 1963.

Supplément au voyage de Cook (1935)
(1) translated by Maurice Valency as *The Virtuous Island*. New York: S. French, 1956.

Electre (1937)
(1) translated by Winifred Smith, in *The Modern Theatre*, ed. Eric Bentley, vol. 1. New York: Anchor, 1955.
(2) translated by Phyllis La Farge and Peter H. Judd, in Jean Giraudoux, *Three Plays*, vol. 2. New York: Hill and Wang, 1964.

L'Impromptu de Paris (1937)
(1) translated by Rima Dell Reck, in the *Tulane Drama Review*, vol. 3, no. 4 (Summer, 1959).

Cantique des Cantiques (1938)
(1) translated by John Raikes, in the *Tulane Drama Review*, vol. 3, no. 4 (Summer, 1959).
(2) translated by Herma Briffault, in Barry Ulanov, *Makers of Modern Theatre*. New York: McGraw-Hill, 1961.

Ondine (1939)
(1) translated by Maurice Valency, in Jean Giraudoux, *Four Plays*, vol 1. New York: Hill and Wang, 1959.

(2) translated by Roger Gellert, in Jean Giraudoux, *Plays*, vol. 2. London: Oxford University Press, 1967.

L'Apollon de Bellac (1942)
    (1) translated by Maurice Valency, in Jean Giraudoux, *Four Plays*, vol. 1, New York: Hill and Wang, 1958.
    (2) translated by Ronald Duncan. New York: S. French, 1957.

Sodome et Gomorrhe (1943)
    (1) translated by Herma Briffault, in Barry Ulanov, *Makers of Modern Theatre*. New York: McGraw-Hill, 1961.

La Folle de Chaillot (1945)
    (1) translated by Maurice Valency in Jean Giraudoux, *Four Plays*, vol 1. New York: Hill and Wang, 1958.

Pour Lucrèce (1953)
    (1) translated by Christopher Fry as *Duel of Angels* in *The Drama of Jean Giraudoux*, vol 1. London: Oxford University Press, 1963.

II. NONDRAMATIC WORKS OF GIRAUDOUX IN ENGLISH TRANSLATION

Novels:

Elpénor (1919)
    translated by Richard Howard, with the assistance of Renaud Bruce. New York: Noonday, 1958.

Suzanne et le Pacifique (1921)
    translated by Ben Ray Redman. New York: Putnam's, 1923.

Siegfried et le Limousin (1922)
    translated by Louis Collier Willcox as *My Friend from Limousin*. New York: Harper & Brothers, 1928.

Bella (1926)
    translated by J. F. Scanlan. New York: A. A. Knopf, 1927.

Essays (listed by English title):

Campaigns and Intervals
    (originally *Lectures pour une ombre*, 1917) translated by Elizabeth S. Sergeant. Boston and New York: Houghton Mifflin Co., 1918.

Racine (1929)
    translated by P. Mansell Jones. Cambridge: G. Fraser, 1938.

"Discourse on the Theatre" (1931)
    translated by Haskell M. Block, in H. M. Block and Herman Salinger, *The Creative Vision*, New York: Grove, 1960.

The France of Tomorrow (1940)
   translated anonymously. Published in Paris by the Centre D'Informations Documentaires, 1940.

"Two Laws"
   (from *Visitations*, 1947), translated by Joseph M. Bernstein, in *Playwrights on Playwriting*, ed. Toby Cole. New York: Hill and Wang, 1960.

III. WORKS ABOUT GIRAUDOUX CONSULTED OR CITED IN THIS STUDY

Albérès (René Marill). *Esthétique et morale chez Jean Giraudoux*. Paris: Nizet, 1957.

———. *La Genèse du Siegfried*. Paris: Lettres Modernes, 1963.

Almaviva. "M. Jean Giraudoux nous dit ce que sera sa pièce, *La Guerre de Troie n'aura pas lieu*." *Le Figaro* (21 November 1935), p. 5.

Altman, Georges. "Allégresse avec Giraudoux." *La Lumière*, 10 December, 1936, p. 6.

Anders, France. *Jacques Copeau et le cartel des quatre*. Paris: Nizet, 1959.

Anouilh, Jean. "To Jean Giraudoux," translated by Arthur Evans. *Tulane Drama Review* 3, no. 4 (May, 1959): 3–5.

Arnold, Paul. "Il inaugure l'impressionisme théâtral." *Cahiers de la Compagnie Madeleine Renaud–Jean-Louis Barrault*, no. 2 (1953), p. 65.

Astre, Georges-Albert. "Note sur Jean Giraudoux, poète tragique." *La Grande Revue*, no. 852 (April, 1940), pp. 174–82.

Barrault, Jean-Louis. "A la recherche de *Pour Lucrèce*." *Cahiers de la compagnie Madeleine Renaud–Jean-Louis Barrault*, no. 2 (1953), pp. 72–100.

Beauplan, Robert de. "*Cantique des Cantiques* à la Comédie Française." *La Petite Illustration*, no. 899 (17 December, 1938).

———. "*Intermezzo* à la Comédie des Champs-Elysées." *La Petite Illustration*, no. 625 (6 May, 1933).

———. "*Siegfried* à la Comédie des Champs-Elysées." *La Petite Illustration*, no. 396 (25 August, 1928).

Beigbeder, Marc. *Le Théâtre en France depuis la Libération*. Paris: Bordas, 1959.

Beucler, André. *Les Instants de Giraudoux*. Paris: Editions du Milieu du Monde, 1948.

Beucler, André. "Vie et mort de Giraudoux." *Confluences* 4, no. 35 (1944): 105–10.

Blanzat, Jean. "Giraudoux et la Résistance." *Le Figaro* 118, no. 30 (23 September, 1944): 2.

Bourdet, Maurice. "Du Roman au théâtre: *Siegfried*." *Les Nouvelles Littéraires* 7, no. 292 (19 May, 1928): 9.

———. *Jean Giraudoux, son œuvre*. Paris: Editions de la Nouvelle Revue Critique, 1928.

Bourin, André. "Elle et lui: chez Madame Giraudoux." *Les Nouvelles Littéraires*, no. 1211 (November 16, 1950), pp. 1–2.

Brasillach, Robert. *Animateurs du théâtre*. Paris: La Table Ronde, 1936.

———. "Le Théâtre de Jean Giraudoux." *La Revue Universelle* 53, no. 3 (May, 1933): 310–35.

Cézan, Claude. "Giraudoux Chez Jouvet." *Les Nouvelles Littéraires*, no. 1018 (May 20, 1948), p. 8.

———. *Images de Louis Jouvet*. Paris: Emile Paul, 1952.

———. *Louis Jouvet et le théâtre d'aujourd'hui*. Paris: Emile Paul, 1938.

Champeaux, Georges. "Comment travaillez-vous?" *Les Annales Politiques et Littéraires* 106, no. 2538 (September 10, 1935); 254–55.

Chancerel, Léon. "Le Drame et le personnage de Lucrèce." *Cahiers de la Compagnie Madeleine Renaud-Jean-Louis Barrault*, no. 2 (1953), pp. 55–61.

Charensol, Georges. "Comment écrivez-vous?" *Les Nouvelles Littéraires* 10, no. 479 (19 December, 1931): 8.

Chiari, Joseph. *The Contemporary French Theatre*. New York: Macmillan, 1959.

Crémieux, Benjamin. "Jean Giraudoux et le théâtre." *Les Nouvelles Littéraires* no. 289 (April 28, 1928): 1.

———. "Judith," *La Nouvelle Revue Française* 37 (December, 1931): 970–74.

———. "La Guerre de Troie," *La Nouvelle Revue Française* 24, no. 268 (January 1, 1936): 132–33.

Dautry, Raoul. Appendix to Jean Giraudoux, *Pour une politique urbaine*. Paris: Editions Arts et Métiers Graphiques, 1947.

Domec, Pierre. *En Pensée avec Giraudoux*. Geneva: Editions du Cheval Ailé, 1947.

Doringe. "Comment ils travaillent: Jean Giraudoux l'irrégulier." *Toute L'Édition*, no. 345 (November 7, 1936).

Eustis, Morton. "Jean Giraudoux, Playwright, Novelist and Diplomat," *Theatre Arts* 22, no. 2 (February, 1939): 127–32.

Fontenary, Elisabeth de. "*Judith* ou le divin intrus." *Cahiers de la Compagnie Madeleine Renaud-Jean-Louis Barrault*, no. 36 (November, 1961), pp. 36–48.

Fowlie, Wallace. *Dionysus in Paris*. New York: Meridian Books, 1960.

Froment, Helène. "Souvenir de Jean Giraudoux." *La France Libre* (September 15, 1944): 455–57.

Gassner, John, "At War with Electra." *Tulane Drama Review* 3, no. 4 (May, 1959): 42–50.

Gide, André. "Jean Giraudoux: *Provinciales*." *La Nouvelle Revue Française* (June 1, 1909), pp. 463–66.

Giraudoux, Jean-Pierre. "Jean Giraudoux et Louis Jouvet." *Cahiers de la Compagnie Madeleine Renaud-Jean-Louis Barrault*, no. 36 (November, 1961), pp. 91–93.

Grossvogel, David I. *The Self-Conscious Stage in Modern French Drama*. New York: Columbia University Press, 1958.

Guicharnaud, Jacques. *Modern French Theatre*. New Haven: Yale University Press, 1961.

Hort, Jean. "Comment j'ai mis en scène *Sodome et Gomorrhe*." *Le Mois Suisse*, 6, no. 68 (November, 1944): 122–27.

Host, Gunnar. *L'Œuvre de Jean Giraudoux*. Oslo: H. Aschehoug, 1942.

Houlet, Jacques. *Le Théâtre de Jean Giraudoux*. Paris: Pierre Ardent, 1945.

Humbourg, Pierre. *Jean Giraudoux*. Marseilles: Les Cahiers du Sud, 1926.

Inskip, Donald. *Jean Giraudoux: The Making of a Dramatist*. London: Oxford University Press, 1958.

Ionesco, Eugène. "J'aime Giraudoux," *Cahiers de la Compagnie Madeleine Renaud–Jean-Louis Barrault*, no. 2 (1953), p. 63.

Jones, Robert Emmet. *The Alienated Hero in Modern French Drama*. Athens, Georgia: University of Georgia Press, 1962.

Jouvet, Louis. "A propos de la mise en scène de *La Folle de Chaillot*." *La France Libre* 11, no. 65 (March 15, 1946): 351–52.

———. "Dans les yeux de Giraudoux." *Les Lettres Françaises* 51 (April 14, 1945): 1.

———. "Jean Giraudoux." *Cahiers de la Compagnie Madeleine Renaud–Jean-Louis Barrault*, no. 2 (1953): 5–6.

———. *Prestiges et perspectives du théâtre français*, Paris: Gallimard, 1945.

———. *Réflexions du Comédien*. Paris: Editions de la Nouvelle revue critique, 1938.

———. *Témoignages sur le théâtre*. Paris: Flammarion, 1952.

Kernan, Thomas. *France on Berlin Time*. Philadelphia: J. B. Lippincott, 1941.

Knapp, Bettina. *Louis Jouvet, Man of the Theatre*. New York, Columbia University Press, 1957.

Lalou, René. "*La Guerre de Troie*." *Les Nouvelles Littéraires*, no. 690 (January 4, 1936), p. 1.

LeSage, Laurent. "*Die Einheit von Fouqués Undine*, An Unpublished Essay in German by Jean Giraudoux." *Romanic Review* 42 (1951): 122–34.

———. "Giraudoux's German Studies." *Modern Language Quarterly* 12, no. 3 (September, 1951).

———. *Jean Giraudoux, his Life and Works*. University Park, Pennsylvania: University of Pennsylvania State Press, 1959.

———. "Jean Giraudoux, Surrealism and the German Romantic Ideal." *Illinois Studies in Language and Litterature*, 36, no. 3 (1952).

———. "Jean Giraudoux's Case against Germany." *The French Review* 17 (1943): 353–57.

Lefèvre, Frédéric. *Une heure avec . . .*, première série. Paris: Gallimard, 1924. (Giraudoux, pp. 141–151.)

Lévy, Yves. "Giraudoux et les problèmes sociaux." *Paru*, no. 19 (June, 1946), pp. 7–14.

Magny, Claude-Edmonde. *Précieux Giraudoux*. Paris: Editions du Seuil, 1945.

Marcel Gabriel. "*La Folle de Chaillot*." *Les Nouvelles Littéraires*, no. 960 (1945).

Marill, René. *See* Albérès.

Marker, Christian. *Giraudoux par lui-même*. Paris: Editions du Seuil, 1952.

Maulnier, Thierry. "Jean Giraudoux et la tragédie." *Formes et Couleurs* 6, no. 3 (1944): 24–30.

May, Georges. "Jean Giraudoux, Diplomacy and Dramaturgy." *Yale French Studies* 5 (1950); 88–94.

Mercier-Campiche, Marianne. *Le Théâtre de Giraudoux et la condition humaine*. Paris: Domat, 1954.

Morand, Paul. *Adieu à Giraudoux*. Porrentruy, Switzerland: Editions des Portes de France, 1944.

Moussy, Marcel. "Jouvet ou Giraudoux?" *Cahiers de la Compagnie Madeleine Renaud–Jean-Louis Barrault*, no. 2 (1953), p. 67.

Moustiers, Yvone. "Dans les couloirs d'un théâtre, Jean Giraudoux nous parle du roman," *Les Nouvelles Littéraires*, April 15, 1939, p. 2.

Neveux, Georges. "Le dialogue Jouvet-Giraudoux." *Cahiers de la Compagnie Madeleine Renaud–Jean-Louis Barrault*, no. 2 (1953), p. 4.

Petitjean, A. M., "Quand Jean Giradoux parle du deuil et de l'espoir de la France." *La Lumière*, no. 612 (January 27, 1939), p. 6.

Poulenc, Francis. "Souvenirs." *Cahiers de la Compagnie Madeleine Renaud–Jean-Louis Barrault*, no. 2 (1953), pp. 29–32.

Pucciani, Oreste F. "Infernal Dialogue of Giraudoux and Sartre." *Tulane Drama Review* 3, no. 4 (May, 1959): 57.

Quéant, Gilles, ed. *Encyclopédie du théâtre contemporain*, 2 vols. Paris: Publications de France, 1957–59.

Rageot, Gaston. "Giraudoux et Dieu." *Cahiers de la Compagnie Madeleine Renaud–Jean-Louis Barrault*, no. 36 (November, 1961), pp. 27–36.

———. "Les Jeux de Jean Giraudoux." *Revue Bleue* 68, no. 4 (February 15, 1930): 123–24.

———. "L'Intelligence au théâtre, Jean Giraudoux." *Revue Bleue* 66, no. 10 (May 19, 1928): 312–14.

Raval, Maurice. "Le dernier message de Giraudoux." *Nouvelles Littéraires*, no. 924 (1945).

Rousseaux, André. "Entre le théâtre et le roman avec M. Jean Giraudoux." *Candide* 6, no. 784 (March 22, 1939): 6.

Rousseaux, André. "Un quart d'heure avec Jean Giraudoux." *Candide* 6, no. 294 (October 31, 1929): 3.

Roy, Claude. "Giraudoux et Dieu." *Cahiers de la Compagnie Madeleine Renaud–Jean-Louis Barrault*, no. 36 (November, 1961), pp. 27–36.

Sartre, Jean Paul. "M. Jean Giraudoux et la philosophie d'Aristote." *La Nouvelle Revue Française*, no. 318 (March 1, 1940), pp. 339–54.

Sieburg, Friedrich. "Jean Giraudoux, *Siegfried*, et l'Allemagne." *L'Europe Nouvelle* 12, no. 570 (January 12, 1929): 39–40,

Sorensen, Hans. *Le Théâtre de Jean Giraudoux, technique et style*. Copenhagen: University of Aarhus, 1950.

Vaudoyer, Jean-Louis. "Jean Giraudoux chez Louis Jouvet." *Les Nouvelles Littéraires* 13, no. 684 (23 November, 1935): 10.

———. "Jean Giraudoux, le Limousin." *Cahiers de la Compagnie Madeleine Renaud-Jean-Louis Barrault*, no. 10 (1955), pp. 3–13.

Walter, Gérard. *Paris under the Occupation*, tr. Toby White. New York: Orion Press, 1960.

Warnod, André. "J'ai epousseté le buste d'Electre, nous dit M. Jean Giraudoux." *Le Figaro*, May 11, 1937.